THE AGELESS WISDOM TEACHING

An introduction to humanity's spiritual legacy

BENJAMIN CREME

Share International Foundation
Amsterdam • London

ISBN 978-94-91732-38-6

Second Edition   September, 2021

TABLE OF CONTENTS

*Publisher's note: This interview is excerpted from Maitreya's Mission, Vol. 3 by Benjamin Creme.

INTRODUCTION

In every age, or in times of exceptional crisis, great spiritual teachers have come into the world to enable mankind to take its next evolutionary step. We know them, among others, as Hercules, Sankaracharya, Krishna, Rama, Buddha, Mohammed and the Christ. Each has given a body of teaching, a central and common theme of which is 'right human relations'. For example:

- ❖ **Christianity**: "...All things whatsoever ye would that men should do to you, do ye even so to them..."
- ❖ **Buddhism**: "In five ways should a clansman minister to his friends and familiars – by generosity, courtesy and benevolence, by treating them as he treats himself, and by being as good as his word."
- ❖ **Hinduism**: "Do not to others, which if done to thee, would cause thee pain."
- ❖ **Islam**: "No one of you is a believer until he loves for his brother what he loves for himself."
- ❖ **Judaism**: "What is hurtful to yourself, do not to your fellow man."
- ❖ **Taoism**: "Regard your neighbour's gain as your own gain and regard your neighbour's loss as your own loss."

From such simple teachings men have historically constructed complex dogma and ritual, willing to kill and be killed in the name of their ideology. Such religious intolerance has been, and continues to be, the basis for much of the discord and suffering in the world. *When men and women of every faith come to understand that they share a common spiritual legacy, as children of One Father – by whatever name their tradition calls Him – a new era of brotherhood and peace will begin.*

This common wellspring of wisdom is an ancient body of spiritual teaching handed down from generation to generation, and known as the 'Ageless Wisdom'. As an esoteric *science* – meaning simply that it lies beyond the understanding or comprehension of the average person – it presents a systematic

1

and comprehensive account of the evolutionary process, in man and nature, from an energetic standpoint: how the universe came to exist, how it operates, and man's place within it. Esotericism, as it is sometimes called, is also the *art* of working with those energies which emanate from the highest spiritual sources. From behind the scenes, these teachings have guided and shaped civilization after civilization, leading to all the great advances in human endeavour, be they in the sciences, politics, the arts or religion.

The Ageless Wisdom Teaching was first made available to the general public around 1875 by Helena Petrovna Blavatsky in her seminal works *The Secret Doctrine* and *Isis Unveiled*. Blavatsky established the Theosophical Society to introduce this 'new' perspective on history and human evolution. The intermediate phase of the teaching was revealed by Alice A. Bailey who, from 1919 to 1949, collaborated with a Master of Wisdom known as 'the Tibetan'. Through a process of telepathic overshadowing, the Master Djwhal Khul communicated a vast body of information about the world and its future.

Since 1974, British artist Benjamin Creme has been the source of further revelations concerning the Ageless Wisdom and, in particular, about the emergence of Maitreya, the Christ and World Teacher for the coming age – information which Mr. Creme received through his moment-to-moment telepathic contact with a Master of Wisdom.

Benjamin Creme lectured throughout the world on this subject and has given hundreds of radio, television and print interviews. Compiled from these lectures, his books have been translated and published in numerous languages by groups responding to his message. He was also editor of *Share International*, a monthly magazine circulating in over 70 countries. He received no remuneration for this work and made no claims about his own spiritual status.

The main article in this book gives an overview of the basic tenets of esotericism and is transcribed from an interview with Benjamin Creme by Rollin Olson, which took place in November 1994 in Los Angeles, USA. Readers who are new to this subject may wish to first review the glossary of esoteric terms beginning on page 62 to familiarize themselves with some of the frequently used terms. For those who wish to delve further into the mysteries of the universe, a suggested reading list is included.

"When you see and hear Me you will realize that you have known for long the Truths which I utter.... These simple Truths, My friends, underlie all existence. Sharing and Justice, Brotherhood and Freedom are not new concepts. From the dawn of time mankind has linked his aspiration to these beckoning stars. Now, My friends, shall we anchor them in the world."

– Maitreya, the World Teacher
(from Message no. 105)

3

4

THE AGELESS WISDOM TEACHING

Interview with Benjamin Creme by Rollin Olson

Rollin Olson: Every day it seems people are talking about how things are out of control – corruption ruining countries, economies in collapse, people losing their jobs, some becoming homeless, the family unit breaking down. A lot of people see no purpose in life any more. Others keep hoping for a turnaround. Do you see any hope for the future?

Benjamin Creme: Very much so. I think that before humanity lies a civilization more brilliant than anything this world has ever seen.

RO: But how, given the problems we have today?

BC: I think these problems are really temporary. They are the result of the fact that tremendous new cosmic energies are influencing our world and creating the present – temporary – turmoil and chaos. Our innate divinity, potential in every human being, is sufficient, I believe, to show us a way out of these problems and to create the conditions which will ensure, not only the continuance of humanity, but the creation of a civilization which will fulfil our every aspiration.

RO: You say "innate divinity". Who are we, really?

BC: We are really gods in incarnation. We need to recognize our threefold constitution: we are a spark of God; every religion has postulated this and has kept the idea of our divinity before humanity for thousands of years. But it can be seen more scientifically and still correctly. Speaking as an esotericist, I would say that the divine spark is so refined in vibration that it cannot manifest directly on the physical plane. It reflects itself, therefore, as the individualized human soul. The soul, in its turn, reflects itself in the human personality, with its physical, emotional and mental bodies. Through the physical-plane personality, the soul enacts its reincarnational process, until finally the individual on the physical plane, the man or woman, reflects perfectly the quality of the soul, which is the divine quality of the spark of God.

RO: What is getting in the way of expressing this divinity right now?
BC: The main thing is that at the coarse physical-plane level there is a resistance, a limitation of expression of our divinity. Hence, the expression of selfishness by most of humanity. We then create conditions − political, economic and social − which further pre-

Benjamin Creme (Left) with Rollin Olson

vent our divinity from expressing itself. When .the changes, which are now under way, go further and reflect the essential *spiritual* nature of humanity, we will create conditions − political, economic, religious, social and scientific − which will allow the innate divinity of all people to manifest.

RO: If we are divine innately, then what is our purpose, what goal are we shooting for as a race?
BC: As a race, our purpose is to spiritualize matter. We are spirit in matter, in incarnation at this relatively low level (although from the mineral, the vegetable or the animal point of view it is a relatively high level). From the point of view of spirit, the human being, with a physical, an emotional and a mental body, is not a very clear expression of divinity. The evolutionary process, therefore, is that by which we spiritualize the matter of our own bodies and, thus, matter itself. That is why we are here: to spiritualize matter, to inform the matter of our physical, emotional and mental bodies with the qualities of the soul, which is perfect; perfect spirit reflected from the spark of God.

RO: People routinely talk about their physical body, about their emotions, their thoughts. You are saying there is an actual body which is the emotions, a body which is the mind, in addition to the dense-physical body?

BC: Yes, indeed. These are vehicles for the spirit aspect, working through the soul, to express itself at this level. Gradually, through the process of incarnation and reincarnation, we do, indeed, create a body through which the spirit aspect can, to a very *full* degree, manifest. When that happens we become perfected Masters.

ESOTERICISM

RO: It seems that what you are describing is not strictly in the department of religion. Am I right in assessing it as a kind of broader view of things?

BC: Indeed, it is a synthesizing teaching. The Ageless Wisdom Teaching, or esotericism as it is often called, is not a religion. It is not, strictly speaking, a philosophy; it is not an art or a science, but it has something of all of these.

You might say that esotericism is the philosophy, or the science, of the evolutionary process, as it pertains to the human and subhuman kingdoms. But it is about the evolution of *consciousness*, not of the physical form.

Charles Darwin

If you want to know about the evolution of the physical form, turn to Darwin – he has pretty well summed up the nature of evolution as regards the *form* of the animal and the human kingdoms. But in terms of the evolution of consciousness, you have to turn to the esoteric – esoteric only so far; for that which is esoteric gradually becomes exoteric. Nothing which humanity can safely use is ever withheld, so it is up to us how much of this teaching is given at any time.

7

RO: Let me clarify a couple of terms before we go on. What is the difference between 'esoteric' and 'occult' – terms that are often used synonymously?

BC: They both mean 'hidden'. That is, hidden for a given time, not for all time – but hidden because, at this point in the evolution of the race, it is largely unknown and unacceptable to all but a relatively small number of initiates and disciples of those who give the teachings. To humanity in general it is unknown, therefore esoteric or occult. The word 'occult' has been given, by various religious groups, a rather bad connotation; it is seen as something dark, evil, to do with nefarious practices, devil worship, and so on. This is a complete misunderstanding of the word occult. Occult simply means hidden, and specifically the hidden knowledge or science of the *energies* behind the evolutionary process. Esotericism might be seen more as the *philosophy* of the evolutionary process, and occultism as the *science* of the energies which bring that process about.

SOURCE OF THE TEACHING

RO: What is the source of this information you are giving us?

BC: The Ageless Wisdom Teaching is as old as humanity itself. This is the teaching of a group of men Who have gone beyond the strictly human stage and have entered the next kingdom, the Spiritual Kingdom. They are the Masters of Wisdom and the Lords of Compassion. They are men and women like us Who have expanded their consciousness to include the spiritual levels. There are a large number of these Enlightened men on our planet, Who have been living in the remote mountain and desert areas for countless thousands of years. From time to time They release aspects of Their teachings, in so far as we can absorb and use them, to enlighten us.

In modern times the major expression of this teaching was given through Helena Petrovna Blavatsky, one of the founders of the Theosophical Society, between 1875 and 1890. Her book *The Secret Doctrine* is the preparatory phase of the teaching given for the new cosmic cycle which we are now entering – we call it the age of Aquarius. A later phase was given through an English disciple, Alice A. Bailey, between 1919 and 1949, by a Tibetan Master, Djwhal Khul, and this is seen as the intermediate phase of the teachings. Between 1924 and 1939, a further body of teachings – the Agni Yoga Teachings – was given through another Russian disciple, Helena Roerich. These Ageless Wisdom Teachings are the means by which humanity is kept informed of its essential divinity, and of its journey of evolution toward perfection.

RO: How did Blavatsky and Bailey get their information?
BC: As far as Madame Blavatsky was concerned, she received it from a group of Masters with Whom she lived for some years in the Himalaya. The Masters have gone through this evolutionary process in which we are still engaged and have learned how it works, what evolution is about. They are Masters not in any authoritarian sense, but masters of Themselves and the forces of nature. They have full consciousness and complete control on all planes of this planet.

Alice A. Bailey

RO: And I would assume that it is from this level of human accomplishment that the greatest teachers of all the ages have come.
BC: Indeed. Every new cosmic cycle – we are entering a new one now, the age of Aquarius – brings into the world a teacher. People like Hercules and Hermes, Rama, Mithra, Vyasa, Zoroaster, Confucius, Krishna, Shankaracharya, the Buddha, the Christ, Mohammed – these are all Masters Who have come from the same spiritual centre of the planet, called the Spiritual, or Esoteric, Hierarchy, which is made up of the Masters and Their initiates and disciples of various degrees. It is also known as the Kingdom of God or the Kingdom of Souls.

9

RO: So this is a state of being, as opposed to a place?
BC: Yes. Christians are waiting for the Kingdom of God to descend on the Earth when we are good enough to receive it. Actually it has always been here, behind the scenes, made up of those men and women Who have fitted Themselves, through the expansion of Their consciousness (and therefore the demonstration of Their divinity).

RO: Is this what the scripture relating to 'the kingdom of heaven in our midst' is about?
BC: Christ, through Jesus, said the Kingdom of Heaven is within you. Don't look outside or up to heaven. It is within you. And indeed it is, as consciousness. If you have that consciousness, you are in the Kingdom of God.

GOD

RO: What about God? Who is He? Where is He? How does He relate to the Spiritual Hierarchy and us?
BC: God, in the esoteric meaning, is the sum total of all the Laws and all the energies governed by these Laws in the manifested and unmanifested universe. So God is impersonal. Nevertheless, that transcendent God is manifest in every aspect of creation, including ourselves. We are not separate from that creation – from God. Every human being has the potential of the knowledge, the awareness, of all in creation that we can think of as meaning God. The Masters are God-realized, which is a very specific state, in that They have brought Their consciousness, in terms of the divine spark, the Absolute, the Self, into complete at-onement with Themselves as men on the physical plane – the personality and the divine aspect are totally integrated.

RO: What about God who is not in the body?
BC: God is also the great Cosmic Being Who ensouls this planet. For all its solidity, its cities and aeroplanes and television studios and the like, this planet is really the body of expression of a Cosmic Being Who gives the planet its life, and Who has a plan of evolution for all the kingdoms in nature, including the human

kingdom. What is really happening is that we, at our different levels, from the mineral kingdom up to the Kingdom of God itself, are carrying out an evolutionary process, which, in its summation, will make this planet a perfect expression of the thoughtform in the mind of the creating Logos.

RO: You mentioned God ensouling this planet. Is there another God or higher level of consciousness beyond that?
BC: Indeed. There is the God Who ensouls the solar system. Our Planetary Logos is only a part, a centre in the body of the Solar Logos, Who in turn is a centre in the body of the galactic Logos. And on and on, galaxy after galaxy. There is no end to God; it is transcendent and also immanent in every part of creation. Every aspect of God, including ourselves, has the potential one day to know all and be all of that, and to work with the energies which create the universe.

God is everything that exists, and all space between that which exists, between you and me, and around us, around everything. All of that is God. God manifests through its creation, which is made of energies at particular vibrational rates. The form depends on the particular frequency of the nucleus and the electrons of these forms. Modern science has been able to break down cellular structures and show that at the centre of every atom is a nucleus with electrons around it, vibrating at a specific rate, and that every atom in the universe is made in the same way. There is nothing but energy in all of the manifested universe. The difference between that totally scientific view and that which an esotericist would hold is that the esotericist goes further and says, indeed, all is energy, but energy follows thought, is acted upon by thought. Thought is the agency by which creation takes place.

ENERGIES

RO: That is a very provocative statement. Can you give us a practical example?
BC: The Great Pyramid at Giza was created by thought. The blocks of stone were actually moved by thought. It is very simple

when you understand how to do it. You create a formula, like $E=mc^2$, the great formula of Einstein which has transformed our whole concept of both energy and matter: energy equals mass times the speed of light squared, the speed of light being 186,000 miles a second. That formula has transformed our physics, and so we see matter and energy as interchangeable. When you recognize this, you can create a mantram. That formula $E=mc^2$, can be changed into a mantram. When you enunciate the mantram in the correct way, you can move objects to wherever you want. You bring the energy of mind to bear on what is simply free etheric energy, surrounding every block of stone and every human being, every fish, and so on. All of that is a precipitation of etheric energy. The stones likewise can be made to have no weight, because the weight is to do with the inert mass and gravity. But when you create the mantram out of the formula and enunciate it, then you can move the stone from here to there. We shall do this in the very near future.

RO: What would you say is the major benefit in understanding that energy underlies all things?
BC: It gives us control over the universe, over matter. It makes it possible, by thought, to be anywhere in the world in seconds. It makes possible modes of communication which are instantaneous, like telepathy. It is the knowledge of energy that makes all of this possible.

RO: So these things are not just tricks.
BC: Not tricks, no. They are the natural ability of all people, only they have to be developed.

RO: And those who have developed these abilities are on the cutting edge of where all of us are destined to go?
BC: Precisely. Telepathy is a natural faculty of human beings. Most people experience it at times; a mother and a child might have a very close telepathic rapport. That does not mean that they know word for word what the other is thinking, but if something is happening to a child the mother will instantly know, she will feel that child is in danger and act accordingly. This is something

we share with the animal kingdom. Animals have that same kind of emotional, instinctual, telepathic contact. When this is brought up to the mental level you have direct mind-to-mind communication. A Master communicates with His disciples by telepathy; He does not usually appear physically. He could be in the Himalaya or the Andes or the Rockies or wherever, with His disciple in New York or London or Geneva, and still be able to talk moment-to-moment.

RO: I know, from having seen Kirlian photographs of the energies around the physical body, that science has made some strides in being able to demonstrate or measure these energies. What about at the levels of emotion, mind, thought? Can this energy also be measured?
BC: It is something which will come. But, at the moment, what we are really measuring is that level of energy which science as yet has not demonstrated, the etheric levels of physical energy. Our modern science recognizes only three levels: physical, liquid and gaseous matter. But above gas there are four further states of matter which are, strictly speaking, material – each one finer than the one below. These etheric planes of matter are the next phase of the material world to be researched and finally demonstrated by modern science. Then the etheric planes will become a reality and more and more people will be born with the ability to see the etheric planes of matter. This is really to do with a certain vitality and with a double focus: you see the physical; you change the focus and you see the etheric. Both are there. The physical is really a precipitation, downwards, from the etheric.

THE SEVEN RAYS

RO: What about energies from, let's say, higher planes or higher levels.
BC: Esoteric science postulates seven streams of energy, or rays, whose interaction, at every conceivable frequency, creates everything in Cosmos. Each ray is the expression of a great cosmic Life, cyclically demonstrating its unique energetic

quality through the vehicles in which it manifests – whether it be a grain of sand, a man or a solar system. To say that a man or a nation or a planet is 'on' the 1st or 2nd ray, for example, is to say that they are controlled by, and express the quality of, that ray.

The idea of the septenate is found at many levels and in many branches of our lives: the seven colours of the rainbow, the seven notes of the musical scale, the seven planes of existence, the seven sacred planets, etc. And, in keeping with this scheme, there are seven ray-types of people.

RO: How do you describe these rays?
BC: There are three primary rays, or rays of aspect, and four secondary rays of attribute. They are usually expressed as follows:

Rays of Aspect
1st ray of Power, Will or Purpose
2nd ray of Love-Wisdom
3rd ray of Active, Creative Intelligence

Rays of Attribute
4th ray of Harmony through Conflict, or Beauty, or Art
5th ray of Concrete Science or Knowledge
6th ray of Abstract Idealism or Devotion
7th ray of Ceremonial Order or Magic or Ritual or Organization.

RO: How do these rays affect the average person?
BC: All of us are governed basically by five ray forces: the ray of the soul, which remains the same for countless aeons; the personality ray, which varies from life to life until all the qualities are developed; the ray governing the mental body; that governing the astral-emotional equipment; and the ray of the physical body, including the brain. These all vary cyclically. Each ray works primarily through one centre (or chakra), and together they determine the physical structure and appearance, the astral/emotional nature, and the quality of the mental unit. They predispose us to certain attitudes of mind and certain

strengths and weaknesses, which we call the virtues and vices of the rays.

For example, the 1st ray of Will or Power has strength, perseverance and breadth of viewpoint. Its vices, however, include pride, ambition, wilfulness and the desire to control others. The 2nd ray of Love-Wisdom has the qualities of love, empathy, the ability to see the other person's point of view. Alternatively, it can produce indifference to others, selfishness and suspicion − according to the vehicle through which it is expressing.

The soul expresses only the virtues of the ray, while the imperfect personality expresses, more or less, the vices. The evolutionary aim is to transmute the vice of the ray into its higher (virtue) aspect.

RO: What would be the value in knowing what rays are manifesting through us?
BC: A knowledge of one's rays provides an insight into one's strengths and limitations, one's line of least resistance in this life, and also an understanding of the bridges and the barriers between oneself and others. Those on similar rays tend to see things from the same point of view, to have the same approach to life, while those on disparate rays find it difficult to come to an understanding of each other's attitudes and meaning. It will be obvious how this factor conditions, for example, the quality of married life or how one relates to one's children.

RO: This sounds like a new approach to psychology.
BC: Indeed. Our present science of psychology is only in its infancy. It seeks to understand the workings of the human psyche and to alleviate the symptoms of stress and disorder. But until it is understood that man is a *soul in incarnation*, governed by certain ray influences, much will remain obscure. It is the soul which determines the rays of the personality and its vehicles. The new psychology, as yet esoteric, will begin from that premise.

15

RO: You have said that the rays manifest through everything in creation. How would this work out at a level greater than a human being?

BC: Well, as an example, every nation is governed by two rays: the soul ray, expressing the highest, if as yet unmanifested, ideals of the nation; and the lower personality ray, governing the people's selfish national desires.

To view history from an understanding of the rays governing the nations and races is to see it in an entirely new light. It becomes obvious why certain nations are allies, while others have little in common and are traditionally hostile toward each other. Or why particular ideas, movements and religions flourish at one period and fall into decay at another; why some countries emerge for a time and become dominant influences in the world while others lie fallow, so to speak, awaiting their time of awakening through the stimulus of an incoming ray.

RO: What do you mean by an 'incoming ray'?

BC: Like everything in Cosmos, the rays have periods of activity and inactivity, ebb and flow. In the case of the rays, these cycles cover thousands of years and are determined by the Plan of the Logos.

RO: Which ray or rays are manifesting now, and what effect does that have on humanity?

BC: The 7th ray of Ceremonial Order or Ritual is (since 1675) coming into manifestation. The 6th ray of Abstract Idealism or Devotion is (since 1625) gradually passing out. Our present problems are the result of the fact that these two highly potent energies are functioning simultaneously, and in roughly equal potency.

As a consequence, the world is divided politically, economically, religiously and socially into two main groups; and these groups are in confrontation throughout the world. On the one hand, there are the exponents of the 6th-ray approach who, from love of the old forms, are holding on to the outworn structures, fighting a last-ditch stand for their preservation. This group forms the conservative and reactionary forces in all fields throughout the world. The other, the progressive forces, are those who are able to respond to the new incoming 7th-ray energies, who sense the need for the new, more living forms through which the new age civilization can manifest. The most impatient would sweep everything away, the good as well as the bad, and need the restraining hand of Hierarchy to produce ordered change.

Under the divine Plan, each ray prepares the way for its successor. The 7th ray relates spirit to matter, thus synthesizing these opposites. Through its exponents, it will bring into expression, as a physical-plane reality, the ideals and visions of the previous cycles.

REBIRTH AND REINCARNATION

RO: Earlier you mentioned that the goal of human life is to become God-realized. Obviously we do not accomplish this in the span of one lifetime. Do we get another chance at it?
BC: Evolutionary progress is based on the process of rebirth; reincarnation is the method of our evolution of consciousness.

RO: How does it work?
BC: Groups of souls are brought into incarnation through two great Laws: the Law of Rebirth and the Law of Cause and Effect. The dominating law is the Law of Cause and Effect, and this can be seen in a number of ways. Scientifically, you can say it is the Law of Action and Reaction, which are, as you know, opposite and equal. In religious terms it is seen, in the Old Testament, as God demanding "an eye for an eye and a tooth for a tooth" – very rigid and very cold and implacable, and a bit nasty. But in the Christian Gospel, the Christ – as Jesus – called it very simply the process by which you reap what you sow; so simple that people forget it.

Every thought, every action that we have, under this law, sets in motion a cause; we are creating causes all the time. The effects stemming from these causes make our lives, for good or for ill. At this moment, we are making the rest of this life and our next life.

We are receiving what is called karma. The Law of Karma is the Law of Cause and Effect. The effects from our previous deeds, good and bad, create the conditions of our life today, and the results of our deeds today create the conditions of the next period of life, either now or when we return in our next body.

The soul magically creates a series of bodies through which it can, *eventually*, really demonstrate itself as a soul. At that point we are well on the way towards the end of the evolutionary process. It takes hundreds of thousands of incarnations, but once that point is reached and the soul, looking at its reflection (the man or woman in incarnation), sees that it is beginning to respond to its (the soul's) quality and is becoming more divine – more unselfish, more altruistic, more concerned for other people and not just for the satisfaction of its own desires – it stimulates the vehicle and begins a process which ends the evolutionary journey – the process of initiation.

Initiation has been brought into life to speed up the evolutionary process. It is not essential, we could evolve without it, but it would take millions and millions more years to get to the point where we are today. There are five great planetary initiations to perfection.

RO: We tend to associate reincarnation only with Eastern religions. Why didn't it get into Western religion?
BC: It did, but it was pushed out. Jesus taught it, and those around Him took it for granted. There are passages in the Christian Bible where it is quite clear that His disciples understood and accepted reincarnation.

RO: Such as?
BC: Talking about John the Baptist, the disciples asked Jesus: "Who is John? Who is this extraordinary man who is preaching in the wilderness?" And Jesus said: "Don't you remember what I told you? He is Elias come again." Another time, when He healed a man of blindness, they said: "Who sinned, that child or his father, that the child was born blind?" In other words, was it the karma of the father, who from some misdeed in a previous life had to have a child who was blind, or was it the karma, some

misdeed, of the child, in a previous life, that required him to be born blind? Many of the early Church Fathers – for example, Origen – taught about reincarnation.

RO: What happened to it?
BC: The Emperor Justinius and his wife did not like it, so they forced the Church Fathers to get rid of it. In the 6th century it was taken out of the Bible, except for these few instances which were overlooked.

But even in the East there is a very uncertain view of reincarnation. Buddhists accept it; Hindus accept it. All the Eastern religions accept reincarnation as a fact. But they see it in a very fatalistic way. If you are born into a very poor family, if you are an 'untouchable' in India, for example, it is because of your misdeeds in a previous life, and there is nothing that can be done about it. You are an untouchable for life, you are poverty-stricken for life, and we will exploit you all the more because you were meant to be poor. So it is as if there should be no change; they accept it totally as a punishment, as the result of misdeeds. It is not punishment. There is no punishment. It is the action of the Law of Cause and Effect; it is impersonal. Social change could end the poverty and suffering irrespective of individual karma.

RO: If we get these repeated chances at life to work our way up the evolutionary ladder, what happens to us in between? What happens to us upon death?
BC: It depends at what point we are in evolution. If we are not very evolved (and the vast majority of humanity is not very evolved), then we quickly come back into incarnation. The great magnet of evolution brings us into incarnation over and over again. Because we have a lot to learn, we need frequent teaching – the experience of life, over and over again – to make any progress at all. If we are rather more evolved, we come into incarnation in groups – family and extended family groups. We have all been mother, father, brother, sister, child, grandfather, etc – in relation to one another – over and over. In this way we create karmic ties. These karmic ties hold the groups together,

and they also allow us to work out, in a relatively restricted circle, our karmic debts – until we resolve them. When we learn to be harmless, we overcome karma. There comes a time when the soul is manifesting so powerfully through its reflection, the man or woman in incarnation, that he or she ceases to make too much karma of a negative nature, and becomes more and more harmless. We can see, therefore, the need for harmlessness in all human relationships. By being destructive we create negative karma, which means we have to work it off. We come in with this karma, and all the misfortune of our life, the pain, the suffering, is put down to bad luck. It is not bad luck but the direct result of our karma.

RO: You talked about the soul and the body. What mechanically happens to each of those in between these incarnations? When we die, for example, does the soul go off to one place and the body to another?
BC: Yes, the body returns to dust. Except that one permanent atom of the physical body remains, along with one permanent atom of both the emotional and mental vehicles. Around these three permanent atoms the soul will create the next body – on the physical, the emotional and the mental planes. We come into incarnation at exactly the same level, the same rate of vibration, where we left off, which is that of these three permanent atoms.

RO: But what about in between lifetimes?
BC: That again depends on how advanced we are. If we are not very advanced, we do not have much time out of incarnation. We are in and out rather quickly. If we are rather more advanced we have a relatively longer period in what is called *pralaya*. Pralaya is something like the Christian idea of paradise. Nothing happens, you do not make any advance, but it is a state of unending bliss which is interrupted from time to time as your 'number' comes up and you are called into incarnation again.

RO: If there is this process of reincarnation and the body, as you say, goes back to dust, what about the different forms of treating the body at death – burial versus cremation?

BC: The only scientific and hygienic way to dispense with the body is cremation, to burn it. Everybody comes into incarnation with a long history of the illnesses of humanity, and some of these go back to the very earliest times. Through the practice of burial, these illnesses, like cancer, syphilis and tuberculosis, are leached out into the earth, enter the food chain and are reabsorbed by animals and humans alike. This has gone on for so many thousands of years that these illnesses are endemic and will take several hundreds of years to overcome completely. Cremation is a first, major step in this process.

We are part of the fifth root race. The first truly human root race was the Lemurian, which lasted about six million years. (There were two earlier races not in dense-physical bodies.) That was followed by the Atlantean root race, which lasted about 12 million years. Our root race, the Aryan (nothing to do with Hitler's notion of Aryan man), has been about 100,000 years in the making, so it is in the very early stages. Each root race has the task to perfect one or other body. The Lemurian race had the task of perfecting the physical vehicle. The Atlantean had the task of perfecting the astral-emotional vehicle. It did this so well that it is man's strongest vehicle, and the vast majority of humanity today are still at an Atlantean state of consciousness, 'polarized' on the astral or emotional plane.

The Aryan race, our race, has the task of perfecting the mental vehicle. We are only using the lowest aspect of the mental planes. There are four mental planes, according to esotericism. The highest of these is called the causal plane, on which is found the body of the soul, the causal body. The soul uses the causal body for most of its incarnational experience, up to the fourth initiation, when it is dispensed with. In this way, the races are brought forward, evolve. Each race has seven sub-races; the Europeans and Americans today are the fifth sub-race of the Aryan root race.

RO: Is there another category for people on other continents?
BC: Yes, there are various sub-races. Today, there are people who are really Atlantean in the physical body, like all the Mongolian type peoples – the Chinese, Japanese, American Indians, the Eskimo,

South American Indians – these all have Atlantean bodies, but the people in those bodies are, of course, of the Aryan race.

RO: There's a lot of folklore out there, I guess, about what happens to us in reincarnation, For example, do we switch bodies with animals?
BC: No. Transmigration of souls does not happen. The fantasy about reincarnation in the East is that you can do nothing about it; however low in life you are, you just have to accept it; there is no social change to better yourself. In the West, some people believe that you go back and forth between the animal and human kingdoms. You do not. Once you are a human being, you go on being a human being until you become a super-human being, a Master.

RO: But you can come in either as a man, or as a woman.
BC: Everybody has incarnations as both men and women. Not necessarily alternately, you might have two or three incarnations as a man, and then three or four as a woman, then one or two as a man, and so on.

RO: Is there a tendency to come back in certain group relationships?
BC: Indeed. We come into incarnation in groups, and these are usually family groups. There are exceptions, of course; there are always new people coming into the family. In the reincarnational cycle, people come into families who bring in different energy, a different quality, different experience, but then are part of that family, and make karmic ties and undo karmic knots together. The whole thing is about working out, within the family, the knots of karma which we have created by our selfishness, our egotism.

RO: What about reincarnating in different races?
BC: We might be in the same race for a large number of incarnations, or we might have a succession of different experiences over half a dozen races. Or we might be restricted only to one race. We might never incarnate in the East if we are in the West, and never in the West if we are in the East; or we

might flip between one and another for many incarnations. It is to do with individual destiny.

RO: So, you can learn the lessons, repeat the experiences or gain the experience you need to reach this point of perfection through different races or racial combinations.
BC: Yes. We are all human beings, we are all God's children, and we all have the same potential.

RO: Why don't we remember our earlier lives?
BC: When we have continuity of consciousness we will remember, but we do not have continuity of consciousness, even from the sleeping to the waking state. We might remember a few dreams, but that is really the activity of the astral-emotional body in shallow sleep. In deep sleep we do not dream at all; it is only as our sleep gets more shallow, as we are emerging out of deep sleep, that we begin to dream, and these dreams we may remember. For the most part we do not remember what happens during deep sleep. Likewise, we do not remember from life to death to life again. Eventually, we will enter the death state completely consciously, know who and what we are and why we are there and what we are doing, and then come back, equally consciously. As you become more advanced in the evolutionary process, this is what happens.

At the end of the evolutionary process, the initiates of the world, who are consciously undergoing the process of evolution, eventually develop continuity of consciousness. They come in because they know the Plan of evolution. They come in to carry out that Plan, and not only because of karmic necessity – although there will be some *karmic* necessity.

THE LAW OF CAUSE AND EFFECT

RO: If people understand, and respect, the Law of Cause and Effect, does that mean they can consciously change their future by what they do right now?
BC: Absolutely. That is the essence of it. When you know that every thought and every action creates a reaction which impinges

on other people, and of course on yourself, then you see the need for harmlessness. When we really understand this basic law of existence it will transform our world.

RO: So are we the only ones who determine what our karma is going to be?
BC: No, there are four great Lords of Karma –They are not on this planet, not even in this system – who administer and organize the manifold differentials of this Law of Karma for the six billion people who are in incarnation right now, and the other 54 billion who are not in incarnation. There are about 60 billion souls potentially able to incarnate on this planet. So this is a major work of the Lords of Karma.

RO: So there's a degree to which we can determine the future by changing our thoughts and actions, but you are saying that there are already certain things set in motion for the planet as a whole that – no matter how hard we try – we cannot undo until they are worked out.
BC: The point is that this planet is not very evolved – not even in our solar system. It is still a 'non-sacred' planet; there are seven sacred planets and we are not one of them. That is why we have all the problems. Humanity itself is not at a very evolved stage, in terms of its future evolution. Even our solar system is not all that evolved. It is probably a quite insignificant solar system, at the edge of the galaxy.

Humanity, from its very inception – and this is put at 18-and-a-half million years ago in the esoteric teaching – has been creating karma, good and bad. Let me make it clear: according to the esoteric teaching, there is actually more good karma than bad karma, but we only notice the bad karma. When our karma is good, and much of it is good, we just take it as our norm, our right. When it is bad karma we think: "I don't know why I'm suffering this." But of course it is still our karma. This has been going for 18-and-a-half million years, so there is a huge planetary karmic debt. Every human being is involved, not only with his or her own karma, individually created, but also with the karma of the human race as a whole. It is not simple.

The Lords of Karma, working from Their unbelievably exalted state of consciousness, can administer not just our individual karma, but our relation to world karma. The Masters act as agents in this respect. A Master can, if He sees fit and the law allows, mitigate the effects of individual karma. It is divine intervention, if you like.

RO: So correct me if I'm wrong, but what you are saying is that, with this world karma, the people who happen to be very fortunate in this life – have all the resources that they need, and who do not pay attention to the problems going on in the rest of the world – ultimately will still have to face them.
BC: Yes, indeed, but that is called complacency. It has nothing to do with karma. Complacency and good karma are two separate things. Nobody is free from the karma of the world. If you live your life, as millions today do, as if the poor did not exist, as if there were no poor nations, as if it was God's gift to the world that the developed world, the G8 nations, should live at the high standard of life that we demand and take for granted as our right, and totally ignore the fact that three-quarters of the world are living in poverty and millions are starving to death in a world of plenty, that is complacency. If we accept that, we are not living in right relationship. The next step forward for the human race is the creation of right human relationships. The Masters say we either do this or we die. We either create right human relationships, or we destroy all life on the planet. That is our choice.

RO: How does free will enter into this set of conditions with reincarnation and the Law of Cause and Effect?
BC: We have limited free will. Our free will goes only so far. Inevitably, the 'cosmic magnet' draws us back into incarnation. Occasionally people write to me, and say: "Please, Mr Creme, would you ask your Master to free me from the need to incarnate at all. I don't like it, I don't want it. I want to get out of life altogether. But I know that if I die, I'll just come back. So is there some law that will cancel the need to reincarnate anymore?" Of course there is not; you do not have the free will to

do that. When you are in life, you have the free will to continue or to end your own life; everyone has that right. But you cannot do it without some reverse. If you take your own life, you have to come back and face the same situation.

RO: So you don't escape?
BC: There is no escape until you have learned to be perfect. I do not mean perfect in the religious sense: being 'good' and believing this and not believing that, and doing this and not doing that. I mean being perfect in the sense that the Masters are perfect, which is having complete control of your physical, emotional, mental and spiritual nature.

RO: What is the best way to avoid making bad karma?
BC: Harmlessness. To recognize and accept that harmlessness in relation to others is the key to the evolutionary process. When we really create harmlessness, we create right human relations.

RO: But why harmlessness? Does it have to do with the inner divinity that you talked about?
BC: It is because the nature of divinity is altruism. The ego is the harmful aspect. The ego pertains only to the personality. The personality needs ego, it needs the desire principle to get to a certain point. If it did not have ego, it would not get to that point, it would not create its individuality; it would be a useless thing for the soul to use. Eventually, a point is reached when the soul can really 'grasp' that powerful, individualized human being, and turn it into a god – which the soul already is. The soul recreates that divinity on the physical plane, as the man or woman, and reflects itself through that. This can only be done when the individual personality reflects the quality of the soul, which is totally altruistic. It is the selfishness, even if, up to a point a necessary selfishness, which in the end has to be relinquished.

RO: Once a person learns about reincarnation and develops some conviction or comfort level with it, does it have any effect upon their attitude towards death?
BC: Profoundly. If you really believe in reincarnation, if it is part

of your consciousness – rather than an idea which you think is reasonable to accept – if you take it quite seriously, it removes the fear of death to a large extent. You may be afraid of the final moments, but the idea of death no longer has the terror that it has for most people who see death as the end of everything and who cannot imagine themselves, this conscious, thinking being, continuing. And yet, after death you have an expansion of consciousness. You are the same being, but your consciousness is immeasurably expanded, because it is freed from the limitations of the physical body. Out of the body, there is freedom and knowledge, joy and experience of love, and you meet again people who had died before you. In fact, it is easier to die than to be born!

RO: I was going to say, it almost sounds like being in incarnation is something of a liability.
BC: It is not a liability but an opportunity for service, for the expansion of our consciousness and the evolution of our being. But to be born is often more fraught with problems and pain than to die.

I have met people who say: "I don't want to come back." They do not want to believe in reincarnation because they do not want to come back and have to do this all over again. Of course we do not do 'this' all over again. We are not the same person because usually we have no memory of ourselves in the previous incarnation. So we do not have all this 'baggage' behind us, thinking: "Well, last time it was much easier," or "I'm all right! Last time was much more difficult." We do not have that sense.

RO: If we do something to set a negative cause into motion, is there any way to mitigate the effects of it?
BC: Yes, we can make restitution, and we can serve to an extent that will counterbalance the effect of that negativity. This is one of the great results of the Law of Service, that it 'burns up' karma.

RO: Looking at karma from a much broader perspective – groups of people, nations, even people of the whole world – are there certain things that we as large groups of people set into motion that affect life on the planet?

BC: Yes indeed, we do this all the time. Governments do it all the time. People like Hitler, for example, set in motion wars which devastate life on the planet for years on end. The events in Bosnia were set in motion by the head of the rebel Serbian groups and the President of Serbia. These two men have an enormous karmic debt to repay to hundreds of thousands of Bosnians and Croatians who have suffered at their hands. Millions starve in the Third World through the actions of the developed nations. Some 40 wars are going on in the world as we speak. These can only continue while the rich nations sell the arms to fight them.

RO: What about altering life on the planet in other ways?

BC: Well, for example, we affect the weather very considerably. Our destructive thoughts affect the elemental forces which govern the climate and weather patterns in the world. If our thoughts are, as they very much are today, in disequilibrium, these elemental forces go out of equilibrium. The result is earthquakes, storms, tornadoes, tremendous floods, and so on, which devastate large areas of the world continuously. This is our own doing. We call them acts of God, but they are really acts of humanity, through its wrong thought and action, setting out of trim the elemental forces. When we eventually come into equilibrium, these forces too will come back into equilibrium, and the climates will return to their normal patterns.

RO: So there are good reasons for right actions?

BC: Goodwill 'pays off'. It is the essential nature of our being to express goodwill. If we express bad will, we reap the karma of that bad will. Goodwill is the lowest aspect of the energy of love that humanity as a whole can demonstrate. It is essential that we grasp this and manifest it as much as we possibly can. Not only that, as I say, to the individual it 'pays off' handsomely.

RO: But it sounds also like it pays off for society and the world at large.

BC: Of course, very much so. Goodwill generates goodwill and is the first step towards manifesting love.

THE PLAN OF EVOLUTION

RO: Where is this plan of evolution going for humanity as a whole? You have talked about what it means in terms of individual perfection. What about the world?

BC: This world is in process of change. It is going through a temporary period of extreme trouble and violence and manifested hatreds. But new energies are pouring into the planet all the time, particularly a great energy from a Cosmic Avatar called the Spirit of Peace or Equilibrium. This Avatar works precisely with the Law of Action and Reaction, which we call the Law of Karma. Under this law, action and reaction are opposite and equal. Out of the present violence, discord, hatred and turbulence, we will enter an era of tranquillity and peace, mental and emotional poise, and an established harmony, which will transform the whole world – and in exact proportion to the discord and disharmony of today.

RO: Where did this plan come from? Is there some place or

The Buddha

being or level of authority where it says "This is the plan for humanity, and here's where it's going to end up"?

BC: Essentially, the Plan issues from the Logos of our planet, the Heavenly Man Who is ensouling the planet. He reflects Himself as the Lord of the World on a very high etheric centre in the Gobi Desert, called Shamballa. The Plan of God issues from Shamballa.

29

It is brought from Shamballa to the Masters of our Spiritual Hierarchy by the Buddha. The Masters seek to carry out the Plan through humanity. They give aspects of the Plan to Their various initiates and disciples, men and women in the world, to carry out, and so the transformations take place, the Plan works out. The Masters are also the Custodians of the spiritual energies entering the planet. They release them in such a way as to further the Plan. Humanity responds to these energies, even though they do not know that they exist. These energies are embodied by certain great ideas which become our ideals. As we put the ideals into effect, the Plan of evolution works out, age after age, cycle after cycle.

RO: How do the scriptures of the world figure in this evolutionary plan?
BC: The scriptures relate to it, but they are usually (although not always) given in a more exoteric manner, in a way that can be understood by the least educated, the simplest of humanity, in a very direct way. They have mainly an emotional appeal for the masses. Over and above that emotional appeal is a very mental and spiritually oriented body of teachings given by the Masters specifically for the initiates and the disciples of the world, which acquaints them with the Plan, with their possible part in that Plan, and invites them to take part in the implementation of the Plan.

RO: People seem to argue endlessly about the interpretation of scriptures. How does one know who has got it right?
BC: The scriptures, if taken literally, very often make a kind of nonsense. But understood in their more esoteric meaning, as metaphor and symbol, the scriptures of all religions keep trust with humanity, keep that relationship between what we call God, the Logos of our planet, and His expression, humanity and the lower kingdoms. They keep us informed that there is a relationship, that there is a Plan of evolution, that this is *not* the end, that we will go on until we create perfection on the planet – perfection being the total working out of the Plan of the Logos, in all of its varied manifestations. Another problem with these

ancient scriptures is that they have all, more or less, become distorted in their slow dissemination over the centuries.

RO: So evolution must be happening in certain steps and that each step has some new revelation behind it?
BC: Indeed, there is a continuity of revelation. Some teaching, like that of Christian groups, does in fact state categorically that Jesus came and gave the top teaching, the end of all the teaching, which revealed suddenly the nature of God to humanity. They leave out of the picture this continuity of revelation, which has continued from the very earliest days of humanity's existence on the planet, and will continue until

Confucius

we are perfected. I believe it is a misunderstanding on the part of the Christian groups to assume that kind of superiority vis-à-vis the other religions.

EVOLUTION AND INITIATION

RO: Evolution is a term that most of us tend to associate with Darwin and physical change. In esotericism, are you talking about evolution in a bigger context?
BC: I am talking about the evolution of consciousness. We take for granted that Darwin has shown the evolution of the form aspect of nature, the physical body of the animal kingdom, out of which grew the human kingdom. The human being is not simply an animal but is the point where spirit and matter meet. The individualized human soul has taken incarnation, 18-and-a-half million years ago, according to the teaching, to enable a higher aspect to manifest.

Each kingdom grows out of the kingdom below it. First is the mineral kingdom, the densest. From that grew the vegetable kingdom. From the vegetable grew the animal kingdom. From the animal kingdom has grown the human kingdom; we owe our body to the animal kingdom. Out of the human kingdom has been growing another kingdom (which we do not even recognize, unless we are esotericists), which is the spiritual kingdom, made up of the Masters and initiates. The spiritual kingdom, or Kingdom of Souls, is the kingdom immediately above the human kingdom; you enter it through the human kingdom. As you evolve to a point where the soul really begins to demonstrate itself through its reflection, the man or woman on the physical plane, you enter the spiritual kingdom through the 'door' of initiation. There are five doors through which you pass to become a Master. All of the Masters have achieved these five initiations. Eventually everybody will become perfect in that same way.

RO: And what are the five steps?
BC: The first step is the birth of the Christ principle. The whole process is re-enacted in the Gospel story, the life of Jesus symbolizing this path of initiation. (Of course, it is much older than Christianity. It is almost as old as humanity itself, and it has been presented to humanity over and over again, in different ways, in the past.) In the gospel story, the birth of Jesus at Bethlehem is the symbol for the first initiation, which is called 'The Birth at Bethlehem', the birth of the Christ in the cave of the heart. That takes the man or woman into the Spiritual Hierarchy for the first time, and demonstrates control over the physical body.

The second initiation is called 'The Baptism', and is symbolized by the baptism of Jesus at Jordan by John the Baptist. This demonstrates control over the emotional-astral vehicle

The third initiation is called 'The Transfiguration', and is symbolized by the transfiguration of Jesus on the Mount. For the initiate, this is the culmination of the lower process that integrates the three lower vehicles – physical, astral and mental. From the Masters' point of view this is really the first initiation, because it is the first soul initiation.

Then you go on to the fourth initiation, which is symbolized by Jesus dying on the cross. It is called 'The Crucifixion'. In the East it is called 'The Great Renunciation', where everything is renounced, even life itself if necessary, to demonstrate the lifting of the initiate out of matter into the radiance of the light of Spirit. Jesus went through it on the cross to demonstrate it for us, physically to set this great experience of renunciation before the world.

This is followed by 'The Resurrection'. The resurrection of the body of Jesus on the third day symbolizes the Resurrection initiation in which the man, now a Master, is freed from the pull of matter for ever. The Master is in a body which is totally resurrected – a body of light. Every initiation confers on the initiate more and more energy of subatomic particles. By the time he or she is taking the fourth initiation, three quarters of that body is literally light. It looks perfectly normal, just like anybody else's, but seen occultly, esoterically, it is radiating light; only one-quarter of that body's atomic structure is truly atomic, the rest is subatomic. This is completed at the fifth initiation. The Master stands free from the physical planet, He no longer has to incarnate, He is now in a body which is totally transfigured and resurrected in the esoteric sense of the word. Many Masters do, in fact, stay on the planet to oversee the evolution of the rest of us, but many go on to higher planets, or even out of this system altogether.

RO: What are the prerequisites for beginning the initiatory process?
BC: The soul sees that the person is beginning to reflect its qualities on the physical plane, the emotional-astral plane and the mental plane, and is becoming more altruistic, that its actions are no longer totally governed by his or her personal desires. The personality becomes 'negative' to the soul, and seeks to carry out soul purpose, even though it might not know it is a soul. Then we see a beneficent person who is rather altruistic, who is really looking for, and working towards, the betterment of humanity; he will have some mode of service, and put others, evolution, and society as a whole somewhat higher than his or her own self.

RO: How long does it take to ascend to this point of Mastery, once you begin the process?
BC: It takes hundreds of thousands of incarnations to come to the first initiation. Once that is taken, it can take anything from two to 15 or 18 lives between the first and the second initiation. The average is around six or seven lives. Once the second initiation, which is said to be the most difficult, is taken, showing the control of the astral or emotional elemental which is so powerful in humanity, the whole thing speeds up, and you could take the third initiation in the same life or the immediate next life, the fourth in the life after that, or even the same life, and the fifth in the life after that, if that is your destiny. There are certain conditions which are too abstruse to go into, but generally speaking the last few incarnations quickly finish the evolutionary process.

RO: And at the finish, a person becomes, as you said, a master of himself, a master over life.
BC: Yes. With consciousness on all planes, and control on all planes, which is another thing altogether. We all have consciousness on the physical plane; it is a reality to us. But few people have control on that plane. There are six billion people in incarnation at the moment, and around 850,000 people in incarnation who have taken the first initiation and therefore demonstrate this control.

RO: That's not a lot.
BC: No, not very many. About 240,000 people in incarnation have taken the second initiation, and about 2,300-2,400 have taken the third initiation. About 450 only, of those in incarnation, have taken the fourth initiation.

RO: How many have taken the fifth?
BC: Connected with the human evolution, there are 63 Masters. But there are many more Masters, Who are working with the sub-human evolutions: the animal, the vegetable and the mineral kingdoms. There are also many Masters involved with the angelic or Deva evolutions, which are vast in number.

THE MASTERS OF WISDOM

RO: What is the relationship of the Masters to us?
BC: They are our 'elder brothers'. They have gone ahead of us and, having finished the evolutionary journey on which we are still engaged, have taken upon Themselves the responsibility of overseeing our evolution. They know the way, the hazards, the possibilities. They know the steps which are the best to take, because there are many blind alleys, many pitfalls on the path, and They teach the correct way. The correct way is the way of selflessness, lack of ego. This is the hard way. It is slow because we are all so egotistical.

RO: Do any of these Masters have names that we'd recognize?
BC: One of them everybody knows, the Master Jesus. Jesus in

Jesus

Palestine was a very advanced disciple, a fourth-degree initiate, just short of a Master. He took the fourth initiation, the Crucifixion, openly, on the outer plane. Normally you are not expected to die on a cross when you take the fourth initiation. He did that to symbolize for us, dramatically, that great experience of renunciation. He is now a Master, becoming a Master in His immediate next life as Apollonius of Tyana, Who opened an ashram in north India, where He is buried. From that fact has come the legend that somehow Jesus did not die on the cross, that He was secreted out of Palestine and went to India and is buried there. It was the *Being* who was Jesus, but in His next incarnation as Apollonius. Jesus is now a very advanced Master. In the seventh to eighth century He went to America and taught the Indian populations, then went out into the Pacific and taught the Polynesians. They all have the legend of a white man who came and taught, and the names are all related to the word 'Jesus'. He taught that another great teacher would come from the East, who would teach the Indians again. So, of course, when the Spaniards came, Cortez and his men, they were welcomed with open arms by Montezuma and his people, who were slaughtered for their efforts, as we know.

RO: You mentioned Jesus. Are there other names that might be familiar?
BC: One, very well known, is the Tibetan Master Djwhal Khul. Between 1919 and 1949, He dictated, by mental telepathy, a series of 19 books through Alice A. Bailey. (Bailey herself wrote five additional volumes.) These 19 very profound, and to my mind very practical, teachings are the intermediate phase of the teachings given out by the Masters for the new age of Aquarius now beginning. *The Secret Doctrine* was the preparatory phase of the teachings, given through Madame Helena Petrovna Blavatsky, who lived and worked for some years with a group of Masters in the Himalaya. One of Them was the Master Morya, her own Master, and another the Master Koot Hoomi, both very advanced Masters. These two Masters are deeply involved with humanity and, with the Master Jesus, will be the inaugurators of a world religion which eventually will develop: a very scientific religion based on the process of initiation which we have been talking about.

RO: These names you have mentioned of Masters are all men. Are there no women Masters?
BC: There are no Masters in female bodies at the present time. The Masters, in a sense, are neither male nor female. They have brought both of these aspects into total equilibrium. On the soul plane, there is no sex, no male or female. There is simply one energy with two poles: one positive, one negative, as in electricity. They are the same energy in polarity. The Masters are perfected souls, so They have brought both into equilibrium,

but when They take a physical body, which not all do (some two-thirds of the Masters today, that is about 40, are in dense-physical bodies), They take a male body at this time to anchor powerfully, in the world, the energy with which They are so strongly endowed, the male or spirit aspect, to relate to the much greater matter aspect as it manifests in the world today. This is to do with the point in evolution reached by this planet. In about 200 years this will change, and then Masters will come in female bodies until there is a balance between Masters in male bodies and Masters in female bodies.

H. P. Blavatsky

It has nothing to do with any kind of bias against women, or the female aspect. On the contrary, the Masters are the stimulus behind the women's liberation movement. They see it as essential that women take their full place in total equality with men in this new age, the age, as it will come to be known, of the Tara, the Mother. The age of Maitreya is the age in which the Mother aspect manifests. The female is the Mother, the nourishing aspect; it nourishes the child, the family, the civilization. Nations are also male or female, and nations which are female may become the seat of a civilization. And so it is essential that women play their full part with equal status in the life of humanity. In the West this is becoming very largely a fact, but in large areas in the East this is sadly very far from being the case. Women are often seen as little more than chattels. A great change has to take place. That is why the women's liberation movement was inspired by the Masters.

RO: How does a Master's body compare to our physical bodies?
BC: He looks the same – better-looking – but His body is perfect; it is a body of light and He can disappear and appear again at

will. He can walk through walls and travel instantaneously by thought.

RO: *Disease-free?*
BC: Absolutely. They do not die; They do not grow old. A Master can be thousands of years old, in the same body. People will soon see the Master Jesus, Who is in a body over 650 years old. Some are in the bodies in which They became Masters. Others are in bodies which are literally thousands of years old. They do not sleep or eat. They live off prana, energy direct from the sun. They are spotless in Their robes or, if They wear Western clothes, very well-cut suits. But they create them by thought.

RO: *Where does humanity fit into the overall scheme of hierarchy?*
BC: There are three great centres, and I have mentioned two of them: the centre which I called Shamballa, a great etheric centre in the Gobi Desert. That is the centre where the Will and the Plan – the Plan of evolution – of the ensouling Deity is known. That works out through the agency of the second centre, the Spiritual Hierarchy of Masters and initiates, the centre where the Love of God is expressed. The third centre is humanity itself, the centre where the intelligence of God manifests. They are separate today but, through the evolutionary process, they will be united. Just as the spark of God, the 'monad' in Theosophical terminology, reflects itself as the soul, which again reflects itself in the human personality, which are both reunited by the evolutionary process, so in the outer scheme of things humanity will unite with Hierarchy. When humanity is ready, when there are enough disciples in the world creating a link with Hierarchy, the centre which we call humanity will be one and the same with the centre where the Love of God is expressed, the Spiritual Hierarchy. That will be united eventually with Shamballa, the centre where the Will of God is known. The Masters are aiming to link up with Shamballa, as we, whether we know it or not, are aiming to unite with Hierarchy. Eventually all three will be linked together, and the evolutionary process will be complete.

RO: Do the Masters work independently or as a group? Do They have a leader? How is Hierarchy structured?

BC: They share a consciousness; They have no separate consciousness as personalities. They can never say 'I', because They have no sense of I. They are a group with group consciousness. At Their head is the Master of all the Masters, Whose personal name is Maitreya. He was foretold to come now by the Buddha: 2,500 years ago Gautama Buddha made a prophecy that at this time would come another great Teacher, a Buddha like Himself, Maitreya by name, Who would inspire humanity to create a new and brilliant, golden civilization, based on righteousness and truth. There are 60 Masters, and three Great Lords, as They are called. Maitreya is one of these three. Maitreya holds the office of World Teacher, and embodies the energy we call the Christ Principle or Consciousness, the second aspect of the Christian trinity. Two thousand years ago He overshadowed His disciple Jesus for three years, and Jesus became Jesus the Messiah, or, translated into the Greek, Jesus the Christ. The Christ Himself is Maitreya. His consciousness, from the baptism to the crucifixion, manifested through Jesus and inaugurated the Piscean age which is now coming to an end. Maitreya has come back into the world now to carry on what He began through Jesus, and will complete in the age of Aquarius which is now beginning.

RO: You mentioned Maitreya and Jesus. What is their relationship with the other teachers throughout history, like Buddha, Krishna, Mohammed?

BC: Jesus taught through Mohammed. As Maitreya had taught through Him, so He taught through Mohammed. The Buddha taught through the Prince Gautama and Mithra, and Maitreya also taught through Krishna and Shankaracharya at previous times.

THE CHRIST

RO: How would you compare the Christ, as He actually functions, with orthodox religious views?

BC: The orthodox view is that He is the one and only Son of God.

Actually, there is no such person; there never has been and never will be such a person. Every single man, woman and child in the world is a son or daughter of God. Every one of us has, in potential, that divinity. There is only one divinity, and we all share it. The only difference between the Christ and ourselves, the Buddha or Krishna and ourselves, is that They have *manifested* Their divinity. They *know* that They are Sons of God, and They *demonstrate* it. We do not know that we are sons of God. We are taught otherwise by the churches: we are taught that we are born in sin and only through the agency of Jesus can we know God.

In fact, God can be known by anyone, moment to moment. You do not have to be a Christian or a Hindu or a Buddhist or a Muslim to know God. You can know God whether you are religious or an atheist, whether you believe in God or not. It has nothing to do with belief, but with direct experience. Because you *are* God, because you are divine, whatever your belief or non-belief, you can know God as an immediate experience in your life – in the way every child auto-matically, instinctively, does when it comes into the world, without having heard that it is born into a Christian or a Buddhist or a Muslim or a Hindu family. It is not concerned with that but with its experience.

Krishna

God is not concerned with whether you are a Buddhist or a Hindu or a Christian. These are temporary manifestations in time and place, and the accident of birth – where you happen to be born. If you are born in the West you are more likely to be Christian. If you are born in the East you are more likely to be Hindu or Buddhist. If you are born in the Middle East, you will probably be Jewish or Muslim. The more fanatical exponents of Christianity, Islam, Hinduism, of Judaism and Buddhism, and so forth, have made these totally artificial separations in the world. This has hindered the

40

evolution of humanity. It holds us back. It prevents the creation of right human relationships. Right relationship is the next step forward for humanity, so anything that holds it back is not something to be welcomed.

RO: You mentioned the "next step forward for humanity. Does that have something to do with why Maitreya is here now?
BC: Yes, very much so. It is a new age that we are entering, the age of Aquarius, and of course this is an astronomical, not an astrological event. It is to do with the relationship now being formed in cosmos between our solar system and the constellation of Aquarius. For the next 2,350-2,500 years we will be absorbing the cosmic energy of Aquarius, which will transform all life on the planet. It is a synthesizing energy: it draws together, fuses and blends, while the energy of Pisces, the age now ending, has separated and divided the world. This process will go forward and, gradually, humanity will understand the reality of its spiritual nature.

This has enabled the Masters to begin to come into the world. It is due to the fact that so many disciples are nearing the first initiation, and therefore entering the Hierarchy, that sets up a magnetic pull, a conduit, through which the Masters are magnetically drawn into the world. They have been ready to do this for over 500 years; the only question has been when would it be possible. It was thought probable that it would be another 12 or 13 hundred years. But in 1945, at the end of the war, Maitreya announced His intention to return at the earliest moment and to bring His group, the Masters, into the world with Him. That is what is happening now.

RO: It is incredible to imagine teachers like this, not just one but many, being among us. Why are They all coming out at this point?
BC: We have reached the end of the age, an age in which humanity has become so divided but has taken a big step forward. We have developed individuality, we have an idealism which, correctly developed, can take us far forward in evolution. Also, as I said, so many have become disciples and are drawing the Hierarchy into the world. But essentially, They have come to an end of a cycle in Their

own evolution, quite apart from the human, which requires Their return to the world. Each Master has done this individually, but now They must show, in group formation, Their ability to function simultaneously on all planes, from the dense-physical to the highest spiritual.

RO: If the wisdom of the ages will no longer need to be interpreted through various people, what becomes of religions?
BC: They will go on, but purified. It is obvious that, with the return of the Masters to the world, a transformation in consciousness is taking place and will continue to take place. The emphasis of religions will change. Essentially they are nurturing stations, to keep alive the reality of the spiritual behind everyday life, and to protect young souls, so that they are kept on a spiritual path. They allow, in that way, a measure of control and of self-regulation of individuals who can, having established that discipline in their own lives, enter the esoteric path and continue their evolution more consciously, as disciples.

RO: Will there be new religious forms or structures?
BC: The Master Djwhal Khul, Who gave the teachings through Alice Bailey, has predicted a future world religion which will be very scientific. It will be based on the esoteric process of evolution, of initiation as central to that path, and the first two initiations will become the goal for the mass of humanity. There will be special schools in which preparation for initiation will be made – it is not something you can teach – which will enable people to take the first and second initiations. Maitreya is the initiator at the first two initiations, and will go around the world initiating hundreds of thousands of people into this deeper aspect of our life. Every initiation confers on the initiate a deeper insight into the mind of the creating Logos, so that you become aware of more and more of the Plan of evolution. If you are aware of the Plan, and of your part in that Plan, you can act much more consciously and, therefore, much more effectively. And so the service aspect of the disciple is reinforced.

THE ANTICHRIST

RO: If Maitreya is the Christ, then who or what is the antichrist?
BC: There is a tremendous misunderstanding about the antichrist, certainly among Christian groups. They expect the Christ "at the end of the world". Actually, He came at the end of the age, not the end of the world. At the end of the world, when the whole world is disintegrating, they expect Him to come down on a cloud into Jerusalem. They think He is sitting up in 'heaven', but the Christ has been no nearer heaven than the high Himalaya, 17,500 feet up, for the last thousands of years. And it is from there that He comes into the world, not from this mythical heaven. Heaven is a state of being. The Kingdom of Heaven is within, as Jesus Himself taught. It is the Spiritual Hierarchy, of which He is a member.

The antichrist is not a man, as Christians believe, who will come out before the Christ, and could even be mistaken for the Christ. The idea comes from the Revelation of St John: the beast, 666, is unchained for a time, and then chained down for a time and half a time. This refers to the release of the energy we call the antichrist. It is not a man but an *energy*, a destructive force which is deliberately released to break down the old order, the old civilization. It was released in John's own day, through the Emperor Nero, to bring about the end of the Roman dispensation, to prepare the way for Christendom. It was released again in our time through Hitler, a group of equally evil men around him in Nazi Germany, together with a group of militarists in Japan and a further group around Mussolini in Italy. These three groups, the Axis powers in the war from 1939 to 1945, embodied the energy we call the antichrist. That destructive force was released to prepare the way for the return of the Christ to the world now. And it was, indeed, in June 1945, precisely at the end of the war, that Maitreya announced His intention to return at the earliest possible moment, and this time to bring His group, the Masters of the Spiritual Hierarchy, back into the world – in Their case for the first time in some 98,000 years.

The antichrist is behind us; it has been, it has done its destructive work, it has gone. Now it has to be "chained down for a time and half a time". This means sealed off to its own domain for the age of Aquarius – that is "the time" – and half the following age, the age of Capricorn, when it will be released again. In the middle of the age of Capricorn the 'beast' will be released once more, there will be another great war, this time fought out on the mental planes. That will be the third phase of the manifestation of the antichrist. It was the war between the forces of light and the forces of evil, as we call them (the forces of materiality as they are called by the Masters), which destroyed the ancient Atlantean civilization some 100,000 years ago. For the last 100,000 years that war has been waged on the astral planes. It was precipitated onto the physical plane in 1939 by Hitler and his group, along with the Italians and the Japanese groups, thus manifesting, for this time, the antichrist. Now it has to be sealed off to its own domain.

The forces of materiality have a role to play: the upholding of the matter aspect of the planet. If they would do only that, there would be no evil involved. But they do not restrict their activity to the involutionary arc, which is their natural sphere of activity. Their work overflows onto the evolutionary arc, where we are, and is inimical to our spiritual progress; it has, therefore, to be countered. The antichrist forces are sealed off to their own domain by lifting humanity above the level where they can be used, contacted, influenced, by these materialistic forces. That is the work of the Christ and the Masters in the age of Aquarius which is now beginning.

RO: In popular culture, and certainly to a degree in religions, the antichrist, Satan, Lucifer, are personified. It makes for great drama, of course. But what is the esoteric view of Satan, Lucifer?
BC: Satan is what we call the antichrist. I just mentioned the forces of materiality. These have the role of upholding the matter of the planet.

Lucifer is seen by Christian groups as the devil. It is nothing of the kind! Lucifer is really the name of the great angel Who ensouls the human kingdom. Every human soul is an

44

individualized part of one great oversoul. The name of that great oversoul, which is divine, is Lucifer.

RO: So who is the devil?
BC: There is not an individual who is the devil. You could say the opposite of good is the devil, and that is in every one of us. It is just the selfish, greedy personality expression of individuals. But in esoteric terms, deeply, profoundly, the devil, or the forces of evil, or the forces of materiality, have the role of looking after the fires of the planet. This planet is a living, breathing entity. These fires are controlled scientifically, otherwise they would explode and the planet would be destroyed. The whole thing works under law. The Lords of Materiality, having the role of upholding the matter of the planet, work with the subhuman devic evolution, the elementals on the involutionary arc, to carry out that work. They are not content with that but overflow onto the evolutionary arc, and that is where the evil comes in.

RO: So, does Hierarchy have to deal with them?
BC: They have to deal with them, and They do deal with them by protecting humanity from too great an overflow of evil, which we could not handle. We are well protected.

THE ORIGIN OF MAN

RO: How did this get so misinterpreted?
BC: Because of the symbolic nature of its presentation in the Bible story of Adam and Eve. Early animal-man, not quite truly human, but no longer simply animal, had reached a certain point in his evolution, with a strong, co-ordinated physical body, a sentient or feeling astral body, and the germ of mind, an incipient mind that would later form the nucleus of a mental body. When that point was reached 18-and-a-half million years ago, the human souls, waiting on the soul plane for just this moment in evolution, incarnated for the first time in these early animal-men. That is the 'fall from paradise' of Adam and Eve.

RO: It was a metaphor.
BC: Indeed. The whole thing is a metaphor. It was not a fall from grace but a deliberate part of the Plan of evolution, that the human souls had to give up 'paradise', living in pralaya, a wonderful paradisaical state of endless bliss, and "eat of the fruit of the tree of knowledge" – take incarnation on the physical plane in these as-yet-animal men. That is what happened, and that has been misinterpreted as a fall from grace: that Lucifer was a great angel but he rebelled against God and thought he was as good as God, and so was put out of heaven. It is a story, only a story, and totally misinterpreted. It is really the story of the incarnation of the human evolution.

MEDITATION AND SERVICE

RO: Is there anything we can do as individuals to help us move through evolution faster?
BC: Evolution is speeded up through meditation and service. These are the two levers of the evolutionary process. Nothing moves you forward faster than correct, scientific meditation and powerful, altruistic service to the world.

The soul comes into incarnation in the first place to serve the Plan of evolution. It is aware of the Plan of the Logos of the planet and it seeks in every way to carry out that Plan. The major aspect of that Plan is the spiritualization of matter, which the soul does by entering into incarnation. On its own plane, the soul is perfect, but in incarnation it has to go through all the limitations of our miserable lives: the selfishness and greed, the misshapen thoughts that we project around us that create the Bosnias, the Rwandas, and the terrible situations in Africa – starving millions in a world of plenty.

RO: What does meditation do that propels a person forward?
BC: It co-ordinates the vehicles and it brings one into contact with the soul. Meditation is a method, more or less scientific, depending on the meditation, of bringing a person into contact with his or her own soul; and eventually into total at-onement

46

with the soul. It is given for this purpose. Once that is established, the person uses meditation as a means of going higher and deeper into the nature of the soul, because the soul is really threefold. It is a reflection of the spark of God, which has three aspects: atma, buddhi and manas. The manasic focuses the intelligence aspect; the buddhic focuses the love-wisdom aspect; and the atmic focuses the will aspect. Gradually, through meditation and service, the intelligence, the love-wisdom, and finally the will of God is contacted and known, and becomes part of the nature of the disciple.

RO: What is the difference between meditation and prayer?
BC: Prayer is often a largely emotional supplication for help, but at its highest is a heart communion with deity. Meditation is the method, more or less scientific, of contacting the soul and achieving union with the soul. There is no emotion involved. Prayer eventually will change and become invocation. God will be seen as consciousness, demonstrating as energy, which can be invoked. This will be central to a new, world religion, which the Master Djwhal Khul said will gradually evolve. People will move away from strictly emotional appealing, into the scientific invocation of what we know to be God: the energies, the spiritual nature of God, which is then demonstrated in the world.

RO: You yourself have brought something into the world known as Transmission Meditation, which you have said is both meditation and service combined. How so?
BC: My Master introduced Transmission Meditation in March 1974 when the first group was set up in London. There are now hundreds of groups all over the world. It is designed to give to the modern, busy, active disciple a field of both service and meditation which, in its effect on the world, is very powerful.

RO: How does it work?
BC: The Masters are the Custodians of all the energies entering the planet. Many of these energies are cosmic and, if sent directly into the world, would be too high and would simply bounce off the mass of people. So Transmission Meditation

groups have been set up through whom the energies can be stepped down. The energies are sent through the chakras, the force centres, in the spine of the individuals in the group. This automatically transforms the energy to a level where it can be readily absorbed by humanity. These are the great transforming energies which change the world as humanity responds to them.

The work is done in such a way as to give the disciples a field of service – powerful, effective – but requiring very little time and energy; and at the same time it stimulates the evolution of the disciples. It is not possible to have these powerful cosmic and solar energies scientifically transmitted through one without the chakras being galvanized. So that when you enter a Transmission Meditation group you are entering a kind of hothouse, a forcing process, which speeds up the evolution of the individuals concerned.

SPIRITUALITY

RO: Some people would say that intelligence is not expressing itself very well through humanity.
BC: It is not lack of intelligence but a lack of spiritual will. We have great ideals, but we tend to think that having the ideal is enough, that somehow it will implement itself. We have to do it. What is needed is applied, *practical* spirituality. For the last 2,000 years we have had many ideals: of brotherhood and sisterhood, a recognition that we are all God's children, a desire for peace on earth, goodwill to all men, and so on. We enunciate it every Christmas, once a year, and repeat it at Easter, perhaps. But in fact, in our day-to-day lives, we are as corrupt as we can be. This is because we have only a *notion* of spirituality. The religious groups are largely to blame for this. Their task has been to teach and to heal. They have taught, to my mind, very badly, and healed practically not at all. And this has separated humanity from its own spiritual nature. The Master Djwhal Khul says categorically that one of the greatest triumphs for the forces of evil, the forces of materiality, is the fact that the religious groups have monopolized the idea of spirituality: whatever is religious is

48

automatically spiritual (whether in fact it is or not) and everything else can be as corrupt as we like. Business is corrupt, politics is corrupt, economic systems are corrupt. But religion is thought to be exempt from this corruption; that is 'spiritual'. We have to understand that the word spiritual means the active betterment of life for all people, for the most people. Spiritual is anything which brings a man or woman to a higher state of life, whether that is on the physical, the emotional-astral, the mental, or on the spiritual or soul plane. Anything which is towards the betterment of humanity is fundamentally spiritual; it is not only a religious thing. The religious path is only one path. So we have to create structures – political, economic and social – which are fundamentally spiritual in intent.

RO: So would you say that the essential role of all religions is to teach right living, as opposed to deifying some figure?
BC: Absolutely. That is what the central teaching of the great Teachers has been. Every Teacher has come, given His teaching to a small group, then has apparently disappeared from the planet. He has been put up in heaven, or nirvana, well out of the way, separated from humanity, and that has left us under the control of the priests. They have interpreted (or misinterpreted) the teaching to keep themselves in power, for the most part. They are the interpreters, they are the link between man and God. Well, man does not need these links. Man has God within him. The church leaders have always taught that God is 'up there', and you must watch what you say and do because God is listening. Whereas, in fact, the God within is the God that really counts, the God Who is taking you forward on the path of evolution, and which you have to learn to demonstrate in Its real nature, which is altruism, love, generosity, caring, and so on.

RO: How does one cultivate spirituality?
BC: Maitreya says to cultivate three things: honesty of mind, sincerity of spirit, and detachment. These sound easy, but they are very difficult, otherwise we would all do them, of course. We all think one thing, say something else, and do something else again; we have little honesty of mind. We have to inculcate, and

practise, honesty of mind. This allows us to become detached. Practise detachment and that allows us to have honesty of mind. It also involves sincerity of spirit. Hardly anybody is who they really are. We imitate all the time. We want people to think that we are this rather than that, that we are nice, that we are good, that we are honest, that we are whatever ideals we seek to present to the world. It is rare to find people who sincerely and honestly are who they are. This produces a state of speaking from the heart and, in this way, the spiritual nature of a person can be conveyed to somebody else, and they can respond. It is a 'heart to heart' relationship which you seek to establish. Then you are who you are. It is like registering and expressing your own identity, sincerely and totally. Again, this produces detachment. These three work together: detachment produces honesty and sincerity, which produce more and more detachment. Maitreya says: "The Self alone matters" (the Self meaning the divine aspect, the Lord). "You are that Self, an immortal Being." And, He says, our pain, our suffering, our problems, are due to the fact that we identify with everything and anything other than that Self. He says, ask yourself "Who am I?" If you do so, you will find you are identified with this physical body, which lasts only for one life at a time and is renewed successively, so it cannot be the eternal Self.

Or you identify with your emotions, your feelings, your energy sensations, which are transient – one day you feel one thing, another day you feel another. They are not the Self. Or you identify with the constructions of the mind, with your beliefs, ideology, whether you are Christian or Buddhist or Hindu or whatever, and with all the traditions that go with that. It does not matter to the Self for one instant whether you are a Christian or a Buddhist or a Muslim or a Hindu, or of no religion at all; what matters is that you register yourself as the Self, that you identify with the Self, which is the same as God. Self-realization is God-realization. If you practise right identification and detachment, you come inevitably to Self-awareness, which leads to Self-realization. It is not a belief, not a religion, not an ideology, but something which benefits all people and is, in fact, the goal of all life.

RO: You say people also develop spiritually through service. Is there a right form of service that people should look for?
BC: The right form of service is that which you can do to your utmost at the given moment. Of course there are different levels of service. Mother Teresa served day in and day out, helping the poor and dying in Calcutta and elsewhere; others serve as prime ministers and presidents of great nations, either well or badly, but they serve; others serve as religious advisers, as counsellors; others serve as teachers, as artists, and so on. There are many forms of service, but they are all to do with altruism. Service is not service unless it is altruistically undertaken.

FUTURE CHANGES

RO: Tell me a little bit about what changes you see ahead of us, and how they are going to be brought about.
BC: There will be a new technology called the 'technology of light'. We will begin to use light directly from the sun. All forms of power used today will become obsolete. This new energy will supply every energetic need of humanity. And, of course, it cannot be cornered by any individuals or groups. It is everywhere, free to all, and is endless in its ramifications. It will also have medical applications in connection with a more advanced aspect of the genetic engineering in which humanity is already engaged. Whole organs will be recreated. Instead of having heart, liver, kidney transplants, you will simply go to a clinic for a few hours and, with this genetic engineering technique and the technology of light, a new organ will be built into the body without surgery. I do not know how many times, but perhaps once or twice per life. Transport will become so apparently motionless, so silent, vibrationless, that fatigue will disappear, and we will be able to go on long journeys without feeling tired.

Also, a time is coming when humanity, just by thought, as the Masters do now, will be able to place themselves anywhere in the world. So if you want to go to Australia, think yourself there and back again.

RO: Do we have to do something to deserve all this?

BC: We have to become decent human beings and recognize that we are one, brothers and sisters of one humanity, and therefore that the food, the raw materials, the energy, the scientific knowledge, the technology, the educational systems, the healthcare of the world belong to everybody, and must be redistributed more equitably around the world: so that we create the reality of the one humanity, the brotherhood of man. And, in this way, we will create the right conditions to deserve all these technological advances.

THE EMERGENCE OF THE WORLD TEACHER – IN BRIEF

1977, July: Maitreya left His centre in the Himalaya and flew to London, coming as prophesied "through the clouds", "like a thief in the night". Since then, He has lived as a seemingly ordinary man concerned with modern problems – political, economic, social, environmental and spiritual.

1978, March: Maitreya began emerging as a spokesman in the Pakistani-Indian community of London, speaking not as a religious leader, but as an educator in the broadest sense – pointing the way out of present world problems. Though highly respected for His wise counsel, His true status was known to relatively few.

1982, May 14: Benjamin Creme revealed, at a packed press conference in Los Angeles, that Maitreya is living in the Asian community of London, and challenged media to invite Maitreya to come forward. The media did not respond.

1987, August: Creme announced: "In the coming three or four months, Maitreya will be working intensively to bring about a breakthrough in international relations." Less than a month later the breakthrough came in the political meetings between the Americans and the Soviets, followed in December by the armaments agreement that no one had thought possible.

Maitreya in Nairobi, 1988

1988, June 11: Maitreya appeared miraculously 'out of the blue' at an open-air prayer/healing meeting in Nairobi. Kenya. He was photographed addressing (in their own language) thousands of people who instantly recognized Him as the Christ. The story and photos were reported by major media including CNN.

Events similar to this have been witnessed by large groups of all religious faiths around the world. At the same time, sources were charged by Maitreya in the near vicinity. These miraculous healing waters have so far been discovered in Mexico, India and Germany. A total of 777 water sources will eventually be found. Maitreya and a group of Masters continue to make appearances to people in a variety of different ways.

1988-1993: Through a close associate of Maitreya's in the Asian community of London, Share International received a series of articles outlining Maitreya's teachings. Sent to world media as news releases, these teachings drew attention to developments which, under the Law of Cause and Effect, Maitreya predicts will take place. Outer events have demonstrated His insight.

As early as 1988, He foresaw the release of Nelson Mandela and the process of détente in South Africa. He stated that governments everywhere would have to give way to the "voice of the people", a statement which found its most impressive proof in Eastern Europe and the fall of the Soviet Union. In June 1988 Maitreya announced that "a world stock market crash would begin in Japan." In 1989 the Japanese stock market lost 40% of its value, and in subsequent years the crisis spread to Eastern Europe, the Asian 'tiger economies', Russia and Argentina. The financial collapse hit the USA hard in 2008 and soon had further worldwide repercussions.

1988 onward: Increasing numbers of miracles have been reported worldwide, manifested by Maitreya and His group as signs of His emergence. These have included: weeping and bleeding statues and icons of the Madonna and Jesus, 'crosses of light' in windows, healing waters, holy text in fruits and vegetables, the worldwide Hindu milk-drinking statues, light patterns on buildings and pavements.

1990, April 21-22: Maitreya held a weekend conference in London for around 200 world leaders or their emissaries from the fields of government, business, science, religion and journalism. Many pledged their co-operation to help implement Maitreya's priorities.

2001, August: Maitreya miraculously manifested His 'handprint' on a bathroom mirror in Barcelona, Spain. First published in October 2001, the 'hand' is a means of invoking the healing energies and help of Maitreya. He says: "My help is yours to command; you have only to ask."

2008, December: Benjamin Creme announced that a large, brilliant "star-like luminary" would soon appear, seen night and day around the world, to herald Maitreya's first television interview. Since January 2009, increasing numbers of sightings of the 'star' have been reported in *Share International*, YouTube website and the media. Benjamin Creme explains: "When Maitreya comes forward, He will not at first use the name Maitreya. He will appear at first on American television, and then in Japan and around the world. He will become known for His analysis of the world's needs. Look for a man who is calling for justice for all the world, freedom for all the world. When enough people are responding to what He has to say, Maitreya will be asked to speak to the entire world."

On this Day of Declaration, Maitreya will be seen on television worldwide via linked satellite networks. He will mentally 'over-shadow' all humanity simultaneously, and everyone (over the age of 14) will hear His words inwardly, telepathically, in their own language. Thousands of miraculous healings will take place. Maitreya will outline the future life for humanity and make His appeal for justice, for sharing as the only way to justice, and so to peace in the world. Our response to this event will determine the entire future of the world. Maitreya has already said: "My heart tells me your answer, your choice, and is glad."

THE REORDERING OF PRIORITIES
by the Master –, through Benjamin Creme

Such is the pressure under which humanity lives today that only the few can perceive the transformations which, daily, are occurring on a global scale. A momentum of change has been established which naught can halt or deviate. Thus it is that the world is undergoing regeneration, purification and pain, preparatory to the creation of an entirely new civilization.

The new civilization will be built upon the foundations of the past, but, necessarily, much of the old must be swept away, corrupt and useless as it is. For those with eyes to see, the new indications are already evident. Wherever men turn their eyes today, a new landscape presents itself, new ideas engage the mind, new structures take tentative shape. A world in flux is transforming itself, the growing pains of change are felt by all.

Into this situation has come the Christ, eager to assist men in their hour of need. That He can help there is no doubt, but men must want the changes He will advocate and implement them of their own free will. Naught will be forced and naught imposed, for otherwise the Law would be infringed.

The speed of change will be conditioned by men's capacity to absorb the measures for which an ailing world cries out: sharing and justice, co-operation and acceptance of the rule of law. Only thus will men find the peace for which the peoples yearn.

To aid men in their task, the Christ has formulated certain priorities which, when implemented, will establish balance and order, and so create the harmony on which well-being and peace depend. These priorities are simple and self-evident, yet nowhere do they exist to any great extent. Enumerated, they cover the essential needs of every man, woman and child. The first priority is an adequate supply of the right food; secondly, adequate housing and shelter for all; thirdly, healthcare and education as a universal right.

These are the minimum requirements for a stabilized world and will become the main responsibilities of governments everywhere to ensure. Simple as they are, their inauguration will have far-reaching effects, and will usher in a new era for this Earth.

The creation of weapons of war looms large in the priorities of many nations today. From this time forward, these new priorities must take precedence, and engage the resources now given over to 'defence'.

When this is done, a great creative wave of joy will sweep across the planet and men in every nation will respond. Co-operation and sharing will become the order of the day, and peoples everywhere will find a new purpose and meaning in their lives. Maitreya will be present to advise and guide, and under His wise direction the world will be made anew. This time is now at hand.

From *A Master Speaks*

MAN MUST CHANGE OR DIE

...My coming evokes in man a desire for change, a desire for betterment, however expressed.
My energies engender in man divine discontent.
All that is useless in our structures must go.
There are many such which are unworthy of man today.

Man is an emerging God and thus requires the formation of modes of living which will allow this God to flourish.

How can you be content with the modes within which you now live: when millions starve and die in squalor; when the rich parade their wealth before the poor; when each man is his neighbour's enemy; when no man trusts his brother?

For how long must you live thus, my friends?
For how long can you support this degradation?

My plan and my duty is to reveal to you a new way, a way forward which will permit the divine in man to shine forth.
Thus do I speak gravely, my friends and brothers.
Hearken well to my words.

Man must change or die: there is no other course.

When you see this you will gladly take up my cause and show that for man exists a future bathed in Light.

My teaching is simple:

Justice, Sharing and Love are divine aspects.
To manifest his divinity, man must embrace these three.

May the Divine Light and Love and Power of the One Most Holy God be now manifest within your hearts and minds.

May this manifestation bring you to the realisation of your part in the Great Plan.

From *Messages from Maitreya the Christ,*
Message No. 81

THE PRAYER FOR THE NEW AGE

I am the creator of the universe.
I am the father and mother of the universe.
Everything comes from me.
Everything shall return to me.
Mind, spirit and body are my temples,
For the Self to realize in them
My supreme Being and Becoming.

The Prayer for the New Age, given by Maitreya, the World Teacher, is a great mantram or affirmation with an invocative effect. It will be a powerful tool in the recognition by us that man and God are One, that there is no separation. The 'I' is the Divine Principle behind all creation. The Self emanates from, and is identical to, the Divine Principle.

The most effective way to use this mantram is to say or think the words with focused will, while holding the attention at the ajna centre between the eyebrows. When the mind grasps the meaning of the concepts, and simultaneously the will is brought to bear, those concepts will be activated and the mantram will work. If it is said seriously every day, there will grow inside you a realization of your true Self.

THE GREAT INVOCATION

From the point of Light within the Mind of God
Let light stream forth into the minds of men.
Let Light descend on Earth.

From the point of Love within the Heart of God
Let love stream forth into the hearts of men.
May Christ return to Earth.

From the centre where the Will of God is known
Let purpose guide the little wills of men –
The purpose which the Masters know and serve.

From the centre which we call the race of men
Let the Plan of Love and Light work out
And may it seal the door where evil dwells.

Let Light and Love and Power
Restore the Plan on Earth.

The Great Invocation, used by the Christ for the first time in June
1945, was released by Him to humanity to enable us to invoke the
energies which would change our world and make possible the
return of the Christ and Hierarchy. This World Prayer, translated
into many languages, is not sponsored by any group or sect. It is
used daily by men and women of goodwill who wish to bring
about right human relations among all humanity.

GLOSSARY OF ESOTERIC TERMS

Age – World cycle, approximately 2,500 years, determined by the relation of the Earth, sun and constellations of the zodiac.

Ageless Wisdom – An ancient body of spiritual teaching underlying all the world's religions as well as all scientific, social and cultural achievements. First made available in writing to the general public in the late 1800s by Helena Petrovna Blavatsky and in the 20th & 21st centuries by A. Bailey, Helena Roerich, and Benjamin Creme.

Ajna centre – The energy centre (chakra) between the eyebrows. Directing centre of the personality. Its correspondence on the physical level is the pituitary gland.

Antahkarana – An invisible channel of light forming the bridge between the physical brain and the soul, built through meditation and service.

Antichrist – Energy of the Will aspect of God, in its involutionary phase, which destroys the old forms and relationships, for example at the end of an age, to prepare the way for the building forces of the Christ Principle. Manifested in Roman times through the emperor Nero and in modern times through Hitler and six of his associates.

Aquarius – Astronomically, the age of Aquarius, now commencing and lasting 2,350 to 2,500 years. Esoterically, refers to the Water Carrier, the age of Maitreya, and to the spiritual energy of Aquarius: that of synthesis and brotherhood.

Ashram – A Master's group. In the Spiritual Hierarchy there are 49 ashrams, seven major and 42 subsidiary, each headed by a Master of Wisdom.

Astral body – The emotional vehicle of an individual.

Astral plane – The plane of the emotions, including the polar opposites such as hope and fear, sentimental love and hate, happiness and suffering. The plane of illusion.

Astral Polarization – The focus of consciousness is on the astral plane. The first race, the Lemurian, had the goal of perfecting physical-plane consciousness. Atlantean man's goal was the perfecting of astral/emotional consciousness. The majority of humanity today are still polarized on the astral plane. See also Mental Polarization.

Avatar – A spiritual Being Who 'descends' in answer to mankind's call and need. There are human, planetary and cosmic Avatars. The latter would be called 'Divine Incarnations'. Their teaching, correctly apprehended and gradually applied by humanity, expands our understanding and presents the next step forward in humanity's evolutionary development.

Avatar of Synthesis – A great cosmic Being Who embodies the energies of Will, Love, Intelligence and another energy for which we have as yet no name. Since the 1940s He has been sending these energies into the world, gradually transforming division into unity.

Buddha – Last Avatar of the age of Aries. Previous World Teacher Who manifested through the Prince Gautama around 500 BC. The Embodiment of Wisdom, He currently acts as the 'Divine Intermediary' between Shamballa and Hierarchy. Buddhists expect their next great teacher under the name Maitreya Buddha.

Buddhi – The universal soul or mind; higher reason; loving understanding; love-wisdom. The energy of love as the Masters experience it.

Buddhic plane – Plane of divine intuition.

Causal body – The vehicle of expression of the soul on the causal plane. The receptacle where consciousness of one's evolutionary point of development is stored.

Causal plane – The third of the four higher mental planes on which the soul dwells.

Chakras – Energy centres (vortices) in the etheric body related to the spine and the seven most important endocrine glands. Responsible for the co-ordination and vitalization of all the bodies (mental, astral and physical) and their correlation with the soul, the main centre of consciousness. There are seven major chakras and 42 lesser ones.

Christ – A term used to designate the head of the Spiritual Hierarchy; the World Teacher; the Master of all the Masters. The office presently held by the Lord Maitreya.

Christ Consciousness – The energy of the Cosmic Christ, also known as the Christ Principle. Embodied for us by the Christ, it is at present awakening in the hearts of millions of people all over the world. The energy of evolution *per se.*

Day of Declaration – Day on which Maitreya will make Himself known to the world during a worldwide radio and television broadcast. Even those who are not listening or watching will hear His words telepathically in their own language and, at the same time, hundreds of thousands of spontaneous healings will take place throughout the world. The beginning of Maitreya's open mission in the world.

Deva – Angel or celestial being belonging to a kingdom in nature evolving parallel to humanity and ranging from subhuman elementals to superhuman beings on a level with a Planetary Logos. They are the 'active builders', working intelligently with substance to create all the forms we see, including the mental, emotional and physical bodies of humanity.

Energy – From the esoteric point of view, there is nothing but energy in the whole of the manifested universe. Energy vibrates at various frequencies, and the particular frequency determines the form which the energy will take. Energy can be acted upon and directed by thought.

Esotericism – The philosophy of the evolutionary process both in man and the lower kingdoms in nature. The science of the accumulated wisdom of the ages. Presents a systematic and comprehensive account of the energetic structure of the universe and of man's place within it. Describes the forces and influences that lie behind the phenomenal world. Also, the process of becoming aware of and gradually mastering these forces.

Etheric Body – The energetic counterpart of the physical body, composed of seven major centres (chakras) and 42 minor centres, a network which connects all the centres, and infinitesimally small threads of energy (nadis) which underlie every part of the nervous system. Blockages in the etheric body can result in physical illnesses.

Etheric Planes – Four planes of matter finer than the gaseous-physical. As yet invisible to most people.

Evil – Anything which impedes evolutionary development.

Evolution – The process of spiritualization of matter; the way back to the Source. The casting aside of the veils of delusion and illusion leading eventually to cosmic consciousness.

Forces of Light (Forces of Evolution) – The Spiritual Hierarchy of our planet. Planetary centre of Love-Wisdom. See also Spiritual Hierarchy.

Forces of Darkness (Forces of Evil, Forces of Materiality) – The involutionary or materialistic forces which uphold the matter aspect of the planet. When they overstep their role and impinge upon the spiritual progress of humanity, they are designated as 'evil'.

Glamour – Illusion on the astral plane. The condition when the mind becomes veiled by emotional impulses generated on astral levels, preventing the mind's eye from clearly distinguishing reality. Examples: fear, self-pity, criticism, suspicion, self-righteousness, over-materiality.

God (see also Logos) – The great Cosmic Being who ensouls this planet, embodying all the Laws and all the energies governed by those Laws, which make up everything that we see and cannot see.

Great Invocation – An ancient formula translated by Hierarchy for the use of mankind to invoke the energies which will change our world. Translated into many languages, it is used daily by millions of people.

Guru – A spiritual teacher.

Hierarchy – See Spiritual Hierarchy.

Hierophant – The Initiator. Either the Christ, at the first two planetary initiations, or the Lord of the World, at the third and higher initiations.

Illusion – Deception on the mental plane. The soul, using the glamoured mind as its instrument, obtains a distorted picture of the phenomenal world.

Imam Mahdi – The prophet Whose return is awaited by some Islamic sects in order that He can complete the work started by Mohammed.

Incarnation – Manifestation of the soul as a threefold personality, under the Law of Rebirth.

66

Initiation – A voluntary process whereby successive and graded stages of unification and at-onement take place between the man or woman in incarnation, his/her soul, and the divine Monad or 'spark of God'. Each stage confers on the initiate a deeper understanding of the meaning and purpose of God's Plan, a fuller awareness of his/her part in that Plan, and an increasing ability to work consciously and intelligently towards its fulfilment.

Involution – The process whereby spirit descends into matter, its polar opposite.

Jesus – A Master of Wisdom and disciple of the Christ, Maitreya who, as Jesus of Nazareth, allowed the Christ to work through Him during the period from His baptism to the crucifixion. In the coming time, He will play a major role in re-inspiring and reorienting the whole field of Christian religion. As the Master Jesus, He works closely with Maitreya, often appearing to people (in disguise).

Karma – Eastern name for the Law of Cause and Effect. The basic Law governing our existence in this solar system. Every thought we have, every action we make, sets into motion a cause.
    These causes have their effects, which make our lives, for good or ill. Expressed in biblical terms: "As you sow, so shall you reap."; in scientific terms: "For every action there is an equal and opposite reaction."

Krishna – A great Avatar Who appeared around 3,000 BC and served as the vehicle of manifestation for the Lord Maitreya during the age of Aries. By demonstrating the need to control the astral/emotional nature, Krishna opened the door to the second initiation. Hindus expect a new incarnation of Krishna at the end of Kali Yuga, the dark age.

Law of Cause and Effect (Law of Action and Reaction) – See Karma.

Law of Rebirth – See Reincarnation.

67

Logos – God. The Cosmic Being Who ensouls a planet (Planetary Logos), a solar system (Solar Logos), a galaxy (Galactic Logos) and so on to infinity.

Lord of the World – See Sanat Kumara.

Maitreya – The World Teacher for the age of Aquarius. The Christ and head of the Spiritual Hierarchy of our planet. The Master of all the Masters.

Man/Woman – The physical manifestation of a spiritual Monad (or Self), which is a single spark of the One Spirit (God).

Manas – Higher mind.

Mantram – Formula or arrangement of words or syllables which, when correctly sounded, invokes energy.

Master Djwhal Khul (D.K.) – One of the Masters of the Wisdom, known as the Tibetan, Who dictated the latest phase of the Ageless Wisdom Teaching through the disciple Alice A. Bailey. He was also responsible for the drawings of the atom, etc. in the books of Helena Blavatsky: *The Secret Doctrine* and *Isis Unveiled*.

Masters of Wisdom – Individuals Who have taken the 5th initiation, having passed through all the experiences that life in this world offers and, in the process, having acquired total mastery over themselves and the laws of nature. Custodians of the Plan of evolution and all the energies entering this planet which bring about fulfilment of the Plan.

Meditation – Scientific means of contacting one's soul and of eventually becoming at one with the soul. Also the process of being open to spiritual impression and thus to co-operation with the Spiritual Hierarchy.

Mental body – The vehicle of the personality on the mental planes.

Mental plane – The plane of the mind where the mental processes take place.

Mental polarization – The focus of consciousness on the mental plane. The shifting of consciousness onto the mental plane begins half-way between the first and second planetary initiations.

Monad/Self – Pure Spirit reflecting the triplicity of Deity: (1) Divine Will or Power (the Father); (2) Love-Wisdom (the Son); (3) Active Intelligence (the Holy Spirit). The 'spark of God' resident in every human being.

Occult – Hidden. The hidden science of energy (see Esotericism).

Overshadowing – A voluntary co-operative process in which a Master's consciousness temporarily enters and works through the physical, emotional and mental bodies of a disciple.

Permanent atoms – The three atoms of matter – physical, astral and mental – around which the bodies for a new incarnation are formed. They retain the vibratory rate of the individual, guaranteeing that the energetic evolutionary 'status' thus far achieved will be carried over into successive lives.

Personality – Threefold vehicle of the soul on the physical plane, consisting of a mental, an emotional (astral) and a physical-etheric body.

Physical plane – The lowest vibrational states of substance, including: dense-physical, liquid, gaseous and etheric matter.

Pisces, age of – The stream of energy, coming into our planetary life from the constellation Pisces, has for two thousand years conditioned human experience and civilization. It was inaugurated by Jesus in Palestine and, at its best, produces the qualities of sensitivity and sacrifice. The age of Pisces is ending and the new age of Aquarius has begun.

Plane – A level of manifestation.

Planetary Logos – Divine Being ensouling a planet.

Pralaya – A non-mental, non-astral, non-material state of existence somewhere between death and rebirth, where the life impulse is in abeyance. An experience of perfect peace and unending bliss prior to taking the next incarnation. Corresponds to the Christian idea of paradise.

Rays – The seven streams of universal divine energy, each the expression of a great Life, Whose interaction at every conceivable frequency creates the solar systems, galaxies and universes. Movement of these energies, in spiralling cycles, draws all Being into and out of manifestation, colouring and saturating it with specific qualities and attributes.

Rays of Nations – Each nation is governed by two rays: a soul ray, which is sensed and expressed by the initiates and disciples of the nation, and a personality ray, which is the dominant mass influence and expression. From time to time, through the activities of the initiates and disciples of a country, the soul ray may be given expression and the true quality of the nation can be seen.

Reincarnation (Law of Rebirth) – The process which allows God, through an agent (ourselves) to bring Itself down to Its polar opposite – matter – in order to bring that matter back into Itself, totally imbued with the nature of God. The Law of Karma draws us back into incarnation until gradually, through the evolutionary process, we reveal more truly our innate divinity.

Sanat Kumara – The Lord of the World; the etheric-physical expression of our Planetary Logos Who dwells on Shamballa. A great Being, originally from Venus, Who sacrificed Himself to become the personality vehicle for the ensouling Deity of our planet 18.5 million years ago. The nearest aspect of God that we can know.

Self/Monad – The divine spark within every human being.

Self-realization – The process of recognizing and expressing our divine nature.

Shamballa – A centre of energy; the major centre in the planet. It is located above the Gobi Desert on the two highest etheric planes. From it and through it flows the Shamballa Force – the energy of Will or Purpose. It corresponds to the crown centre (chakra).

Solar Logos – Divine Being ensouling our solar system.

Soul (Ego, Higher Self, inner ruler, Christ within, Son of Mind, Solar Angel) – The linking principle between Spirit and matter; between God and His form. Provides consciousness, character and quality to all manifestation in form.

Spirit – As used by Maitreya, a term meaning the sum total of all the energies – the life force – animating and vitalizing an individual. Also used, more esoterically, to mean the Monad which reflects itself in the soul.

Spirit of Peace or Equilibrium – A cosmic Being Who assists the work of Maitreya by overshadowing Him with His energy. He works closely with the Law of Action and Reaction, to transform the present chaotic conditions into the opposite state in exact proportion.

Spiritual – The quality of any activity which drives the human being forward towards some form of development – physical, emotional, intuitional, social – in advance of his or her present state.

Spiritual Hierarchy (White Brotherhood, Society of Illumined Minds) – The Kingdom of God, the Spiritual Kingdom or the Kingdom of souls, made up of the Masters and initiates of all degrees and Whose purpose is to implement the Plan of God. Planetary centre of Love-Wisdom.

Three Spiritual Festivals – Determined by the full moons of Aries, Taurus and Gemini (April, May and June). These festivals, celebrated as the Easter, Wesak and Christ Festivals, will be central to the New World Religion and will constitute, each of them, a great Approach of Deity – the evocation of the Divine Light, Divine Love, and Divine Will, which can then be anchored on the Earth and utilised by man.

Transmission Meditation – A group meditation for the purpose of 'stepping down' (transforming) spiritual energies emanating from the Spiritual Hierarchy of Masters which thus become accessible and useful to the general public. It is the creation of a vortex or pool of higher energy for the benefit of humanity. This is a form of service which is simple to do, and is at the same time a powerful means of personal growth. There are hundreds of Transmission Meditation groups active in many countries around the world.

Triangle – In meditation, three people, the minimum needed to transmit spiritual energies. Also, a group of three people who link up each day in thought for a few minutes of creative meditation.

Vehicle – The form by means of which higher beings find expression on the lower planes. The physical, astral and mental bodies, for instance, form the vehicles of the soul on lower levels.

Vibration – Movement of energy. All energy vibrates at its own particular frequency. The evolutionary process proceeds through a heightening of the vibrational rate in response to higher incoming energies.

World Teacher – The head of the Spiritual Hierarchy in any given cycle. The Master of all the Masters. The office held at present by the Lord Maitreya.

Yoga – Union of the lower nature with the higher. Also, different forms and techniques to gain control of the physical, astral or mental bodies.

BOOKS BY BENJAMIN CREME
Listed in order of publication

The Reappearance of the Christ and the Masters of Wisdom

In his first book, Benjamin Creme gives the background and pertinent information concerning the emergence of Maitreya (the Christ), as World Teacher for the New Age now dawning. Expected under different names by all religious groups, Maitreya comes to help us create co-operation among the many ideological factions, galvanize world goodwill and sharing, and inspire sweeping political, social, economic and environmental reforms. Benjamin Creme puts the most profound event of the last 2,000 years into its correct historical and esoteric context and describes what effect the World Teacher's presence will have on both the world's institutions and the average person. Through his telepathic contact with a Master of Wisdom, Creme offers insights on such subjects as the soul and reincarnation, fear of death, telepathy, meditation, nuclear energy, ancient civilizations, UFOs, problems of the developing world, a new economic order, and the antichrist.

Messages from Maitreya the Christ

During the years of preparation for His emergence, Maitreya gave 140 Messages through Benjamin Creme during public lectures in London from 1977 to 1982. The method used was mental overshadowing and a telepathic rapport thus set up.

Maitreya's Messages of sharing, co-operation and unity inspire readers to spread the news of His reappearance and to work urgently for the rescue of millions suffering from poverty and starvation in a world of plenty. In Message No. 11 Maitreya says: "My Plan is to show you that the way out of your problems is to listen again to the true voice of God within your hearts, to share the produce of this most bountiful of worlds among your brothers and sisters everywhere...."

Maitreya's words are a unique source of wisdom, hope and succour at this critical time of world change, and when read aloud

74

these profound yet simple Messages invoke His energy and blessing.

Transmission: A Meditation for the New Age

Transmission Meditation is a form of group meditation for the purpose of 'stepping down' (transforming) spiritual energies which thus become accessible and useful to the general public. It is the creation, in co-operation with the Hierarchy of Masters, of a vortex or pool of higher energy for the benefit of humanity.

Introduced in 1974 by Benjamin Creme, under the direction of his Master, this is a form of service which is simple to do and is at the same time a powerful means of personal growth. The meditation is a combination of two yogas: Karma Yoga (yoga of service) and Laya Yoga (yoga of energy or chakras). It is a service in which we can be involved for the rest of our lives knowing that we are helping the evolution of humanity into, and beyond, the New Age. There are hundreds of Transmission Meditation groups active in many countries around the world.

In this practical and inspiring book Benjamin Creme describes the aims, technique and results of Transmission Meditation, as well as the underlying purpose of the meditation for the development of disciples.

A Master Speaks, Volumes One and Two

Humanity is guided from behind the scenes by a highly evolved and illumined group of men Who have preceded us along the path of evolution. These Masters of Wisdom, as They are called, seldom appear openly, but usually work through Their disciples – men and women who influence society through their work in science, education, art, religion, politics, and in every department of life.

British artist Benjamin Creme was a disciple of a Master with Whom he was in close telepathic contact. Since the launching of Share International, the magazine of which Benjamin Creme was editor, his Master has contributed to every issue an inspiring article on a wide range of subjects: reason and intuition, the new civilization, health and healing, the art of living, the need for synthesis, justice, the Son of Man, human rights, the law of rebirth, the end of hunger, sharing for peace, the rise of people power, the brightest future, co-operation – and many more.

The major purpose of these articles is to draw attention to the needs of the present and the immediate future time, and to give information about the teachings of Maitreya, the Master of all the Masters. Volume One contains 223 articles from the first 22 volumes of Share International. Volume Two contains the remaining 118 articles.

Maitreya's Mission, Volume One

The first of a trilogy of books which describe the emergence and teachings of Maitreya, the World Teacher. As human consciousness steadily matures, many of the ancient 'mysteries' are now being revealed. This volume can be seen as a guidebook for humanity as it travels on the evolutionary journey. The book's canvas is vast: from the new teachings of the Christ to meditation and karma, from life after death and reincarnation to healing and social transformation, from initiation and the role of service to the Seven Rays, from Leonardo da Vinci and Mozart to Sathya Sai Baba. It sets the scene and prepares the way for the work of Maitreya, as World Teacher, and the creation of a new and better life for all. It is a powerful message of hope.

Maitreya's Mission, Volume Two

This inspiring and heart-warming book offers new hope and guidance to a suffering world on the threshold of a Golden Age. It presents the teachings of Maitreya, the World Teacher, on both the outer (practical) and inner (spiritual) levels; His uniquely accurate forecasts of world events, which have astonished international media; and His miraculous appearances which have brought hope and inspiration to many thousands. It also contains a series of unique interviews with Benjamin Creme's Master which throw new and revealing light on some of the greatest problems facing humanity.

This book covers an enormous range: Maitreya's teachings, the growth of consciousness, new forms of government, commercialization and market forces, the Principle of Sharing, life in the New Age, schools without walls, the Technology of Light, crop circles, the Self, telepathy, disease and death, energy and thought, Transmission Meditation, the soul's purpose. Also includes transcripts of Benjamin Creme's inspiring talks on 'The Overcoming of Fear' and 'The Call to Service'.

The Ageless Wisdom Teaching

An overview of humanity's spiritual legacy, this book is a concise and easy-to-understand introduction to the Ageless Wisdom Teaching. It explains the basic tenets of esotericism, including: the source of the Teaching, the origin of man, the Plan of evolution, rebirth and reincarnation, and the Law of Cause and Effect (karma). Also included is an esoteric glossary and a recommended reading list.

Maitreya's Mission, Volume Three

Benjamin Creme presents a compelling vision of the future. With Maitreya, the World Teacher, and His disciples, the Masters of Wisdom, openly offering Their guidance, humanity will create a civilization worthy of its divine potential. Peace will be established; sharing the world's resources the norm; maintaining our environment a top priority. The new education will teach the fact of the soul and the evolution of consciousness. The cities of the world will be transformed into centres of great beauty.

This book offers invaluable wisdom on a vast range of topics. It includes Maitreya's priorities for the future, and an interview with a Master of Wisdom on 'The Challenge of the 21st Century'. It explores karma and reincarnation, the origin of humanity, meditation and service, the Plan of Evolution, and other fundamental concepts of the Ageless Wisdom Teachings. It includes a fascinating look, from an esoteric, spiritual perspective at ten famous artists – among them Leonardo da

Vinci, Michelangelo and Rembrandt – by Benjamin Creme, himself an artist.

Like the first two volumes of Maitreya's Mission, this work combines profound spiritual truths with practical solutions to today's most vexing problems. It is indeed a message of hope for a humanity ready to "begin the creation of a civilization such as this world has never yet seen".

The Great Approach: New Light and Life for Humanity

Addresses the problems of our chaotic world and its gradual change under the influence of a group of perfected men, the Masters of Wisdom, Who, with Their leader Maitreya, the World Teacher, are returning openly to the world for the first time in 98,000 years.

The book covers such topics as: sharing, the USA in a quandary, ethnic conflicts, crime and violence, environment and pollution, genetic engineering, science and religion, the nature of light, health and healing, education, miracles, the soul and incarnation. An extraordinary synthesis of knowledge, it throws a searchlight on the future; with clear vision it predicts our highest achievements of thought to reveal the amazing scientific discoveries which lie ahead. It shows us a world in which war is a thing of the past, and the needs of all are met.

The Art of Co-operation

Deals with the most pressing problems of our time, and their solution, from the point of view of the Ageless Wisdom Teachings that, for millennia, have revealed the forces underlying the outer world. Benjamin Creme brings these teachings up to date, preparing the way for the imminent emergence of Maitreya, the World Teacher, and His group of Masters of Wisdom.

This volume looks at a world locked in ancient competition, trying to solve its problems by old and out-worn methods, while the answer – co-operation – lies in our own hands. It shows the way to a world of justice, freedom and peace through a growing appreciation of the unity underlying all life. Maitreya will inspire in us this growing realization.

Topics include: the necessity of co-operation, the USA and competition, organism versus organization, opportunity for service, fear of loss, karma, love, courage and detachment, overcoming of glamour, how the Masters teach, unity in diversity, consensus, trust.

Maitreya's Teachings: The Laws of Life

We do not have even fragments of the teachings of former World Teachers given prior to certain knowledge of Their existence. We do not have the teachings of a Christ, or a Buddha, or a Krishna, except seen through the eyes of later followers. For the first time we are given the flavour of the thoughts and insights of a Being of immeasurable stature to enable us to understand the path of evolution stretching ahead of us which He has come to outline for us. The impression left in the mind by the Teacher is that the breadth and depth of His knowledge and awareness have no limits; that He is tolerant and wise beyond conception, and of amazing humility.

Few could read from these pages without being changed. To some the extraordinary insights into world events will be of major interest, while to others the laying bare of the secrets of Self-realization, the simple description of experienced truth, will be a revelation. To anyone seeking to understand the Laws of Life, Maitreya's wisdom will take them quickly to the core of Life itself, and provide them with a simple path stretching to the mountain-top. The essential unity of all life is underscored in a clear and meaningful way. Never, it would appear, have the Laws by which we live seemed so natural and so unconstraining.

The Art of Living: Living Within the Laws of Life

Inspired by the writings of two Masters of Wisdom – the Master Djwhal Khul and, particularly, Benjamin Creme's own Master – Part One of this book considers the experience of living as a form of art, like painting or music. To reach a high level of expression requires both knowledge of and adherence to certain fundamental principles. In the art of life, it is through the understanding of the great Law of Cause and Effect, and the related Law of Rebirth, that we achieve the poised harmlessness that leads to personal happiness, right human relations and the correct path for all humanity on its evolutionary journey.

Parts Two and Three, 'The Pairs of Opposites' and 'Illusion', propose that it is man's unique position in the evolutionary scheme – the meeting point of spirit and matter – that produces his seemingly endless struggle both within himself and in outer living. The means by which he emerges from the fog of illusion, and blends these two aspects of himself into one perfect Whole, is living life itself with growing detachment and objective self-awareness.

The World Teacher for All Humanity

Maitreya, the World Teacher, stands poised, ready to emerge into full public work. This book presents an overview of this momentous event: the return to the everyday world of Maitreya in July 1977 and the gradual emergence of His group, the Masters of Wisdom; the enormous changes that Maitreya's presence has brought about; and His plans, priorities and recommendations for the immediate future. It discusses in detail the quality and capacity of Maitreya based on a series of articles written by Benjamin Creme's Master – Maitreya as a great spiritual Avatar with immeasurable love, wisdom and power; and as a friend and brother of humanity who is here to lead the whole of humanity into the new age of Aquarius.

The Awakening of Humanity

A companion volume to The World Teacher for All Humanity, which emphasizes the nature of Maitreya as World Teacher, the Embodiment of Love and Wisdom.

The Awakening of Humanity focuses on the day when Maitreya declares Himself openly as World Teacher for the age of Aquarius. It describes the process of Maitreya's emergence, the steps leading to the Day of Declaration, and humanity's response to this momentous experience.

Of the Day of Declaration Benjamin Creme's Master says: "Never before will men have heard the call to their divinity, the challenge to their presence here on Earth. Each, singly and solemnly alone, will know for that time the purpose and meaning of their lives, will experience anew the grace of childhood, the purity of aspiration cleansed of self. For these precious minutes, men will know afresh the joy of full participation in the realities of Life, will feel connected one to another, like the memory of a distant past."

The Gathering of the Forces of Light: UFOs and Their Spiritual Mission

This is a book about UFOs, but with a difference. It is written by someone who has worked with them and knows about them from the inside. Benjamin Creme sees the presence of UFOs as planned and of immense value for the people of Earth.

According to Benjamin Creme, the UFOs and the people in them are engaged on a spiritual mission to ease humanity's lot and to save this planet from further and faster destruction. Our own planetary Hierarchy, led by Maitreya, the World Teacher, now living among us, works tirelessly with their Space Brothers in a fraternal enterprise to restore sanity to this Earth.

Topics covered in this unique book include: the Space Brothers' work on Earth; George Adamski; crop circles; the new Technology of Light; Benjamin Creme's work with the Space Brothers; the dangers of nuclear radiation; saving the planet; the 'star' heralding Maitreya's emergence; Maitreya's first interview; education in the New Age; intuition and creativity; family and karma.

Part One 'UFOs and Their Spiritual Mission'; Part Two 'Education in the New Age'.

81

Unity in Diversity: The Way Ahead for Humanity

We need a new, hopeful vision for the future. This book presents such a vision: a future that embraces a world at peace in harmony and unity, while each individual quality and approach is welcomed and needed. It is visionary, but is expressed with a cogent and compelling logic.

This book concerns the future of every man, woman and child. It is about the future of the Earth itself. Humanity, Creme says, is at a crossroads and has a major decision to make: to go onwards and create a brilliant new civilisation in which all are free and social justice reigns, or continue as we are, divided and competing, and see the end of life on planet Earth. Creme writes for the Spiritual Hierarchy on Earth, whose Plan for the betterment of all humanity he presents. He shows that the path forward for us all is the realisation of our essential unity without the sacrifice of our equally essential diversity.

The Esoteric Art of Benjamin Creme

This book includes 30 illustrations of Benjamin Creme's most iconic paintings, which he describes as 'modern mandalas' that can symbolically represent aspects of the universe and, through their release of the energy contained in their forms, can be used as objects for meditation and greater enlightenment. He further comments on their concept, colour, meaning and esoteric significance.

Benjamin Creme's art is far in advance of its time and, as such, his work is revelatory. It can be experienced at a deep intuitive level and enjoyed for its energy, power, scope and exquisite sensitivity. Each work affords the viewer an experience – a still point of reflection or meditation – lifting one into a higher, quieter state which has the power to transform both the viewer and his sense of everyday reality.

~ ~ ~

Benjamin Creme's books have been translated and published in Dutch, French, German, Japanese and Spanish by groups responding to this message. Some have also been published in Chinese, Croatian, Finnish, Greek, Hebrew, Italian, Portuguese, Romanian, Russian, Slovenian and Swedish. Further translations are planned. Books are available from local booksellers, online vendors and the publisher.

SHARE INTERNATIONAL MAGAZINE
ISSN 0169-1341

A unique magazine featuring each month: up-to-date information about the emergence of Maitreya, the World Teacher; an article from a Master of Wisdom; expansions of the esoteric teachings; Benjamin Creme's answers to a wide variety of topical and esoteric questions; articles by and interviews with people at the forefront of progressive world change; news from UN agencies and reports of positive developments in the transformation of our world.

Share International brings together the two major directions of New Age thinking: the political and the spiritual. It shows the synthesis underlying the political, social, economic and spiritual changes now occurring on a global scale, and seeks to stimulate practical action to rebuild our world along more just and compassionate lines.

Share International covers news, events and comments related to Maitreya's priorities: an adequate supply of the right food, housing and shelter for all, healthcare and education as universal rights, and the maintenance of ecological balance in the world.

Versions of *Share International* are available in Dutch, French, German, Japanese and Slovenian. For subscription information, contact the appropriate office below.

**For North, Central and South America, Australia,
New Zealand and the Philippines**
Share International
PO Box 19556, Boulder, CO 80308 USA

For the UK
Share International
PO Box 3677, London NW5 1RU, UK

For the rest of the world
Share International
PO Box 41877, 1009 DB Amsterdam, Holland

For more information: **www.share-international.org**

RECOMMENDED READING

Vera Stanley Alder: *The Initiation of the World* (1939); *Humanity Comes of Age* (1950). Rider, London.

Alice A. Bailey: Various works including: *Initiation, Human and Solar* (1922); *The Reappearance of the Christ* (1948); *The Externalisation of the Hierarchy* (1957); *Ponder on This* (1971). Lucis Publishing Co, New York.

Annie Besant: *Esoteric Christianity.* Theosophical Publishing House, Wheaton, IL, USA, 1989.

H.P. Blavatsky: Various titles including: *The Secret Doctrine* (1888); *Isis Unveiled* (1877). Theosophical Publishing House, London.

Manly P. Hall: *Secret Teachings of all Ages.* Philosophical Research Society, Los Angeles, USA, 1994.

Aart Jurriaanse: *Bridges.* Bridges Trust, Pretoria, South Africa, 1978. *Prophecies.* World Unity and Service, Inc, Craighall, South Africa, 1977.

J. Krishnamurti: Various works including: *Commentaries on Living, Series 1-3.* Theosophical Publishing House, Wheaton, IL, USA, 1992. *The First and Last Freedom* (1975); *Education and the Significance of Life* (1982). Harper & Row, New York, USA.

C.W. Leadbeater: Various works including: *The Masters and the Path* (1973); *Man, Visible and Invisible* (1971); *The Inner Life* (1978). Theosophical Publishing House, Wheaton, IL, USA.

M. Macdonald-Bayne: *Beyond the Himalayas.* Fowler & Co, London. (Reprinted Mystica Publications, Christchurch, New Zealand, 2002.)

Howard Murphet: *Walking the Path With Sai Baba.* Samuel Weiser, York Beach, ME, USA, 1993.

Swami Omananda: *Towards the Mysteries.* Neville Spearman, London, 1968.

Helena Roerich: Various works including: *Leaves of Morya's Garden, Vol. I: The Call* (1924); *Leaves of Morya's Garden, Vol. II: Illumination* (1925). Agni Yoga Society, New York.

A.P. Sinnett: *The Mahatma Letters.* Theosophical University Press, Pasadena, CA, USA, 1992; *Esoteric Buddhism*, Originally published in 1883 with 153 subsequent editions.

Baird T. Spalding: *Life and Teachings of the Masters of the Far East.* DeVorss & Co, Marina del Rey, CA, USA, 1924.

Paramahansa Yogananda: *Autobiography of a Yogi.* Self-Realization Fellowship, Los Angeles, USA, 1972.

ABOUT THE AUTHOR

Born on 5 December 1922 in Glasgow, Scotland, painter and esotericist Benjamin Creme dedicated much of his life to preparing the world for the most extraordinary event in human history – the return to the everyday world of our spiritual mentors, the Spiritual Hierarchy of Masters with at Their head Maitreya, the World Teacher.

Working under the tutelage of one of the Masters of Wisdom, Benjamin Creme dedicated the last 40 years of his life to this work and in doing so inspired hundreds of thousands of people across the world. He began his public mission in 1974 and lectured worldwide from 1979 onwards, only finally stopping at the age of 91. Benjamin Creme appeared on television, radio and in documentary films worldwide and lectured throughout Western and Eastern Europe, the USA, Japan, Taiwan, Australia, New Zealand, Canada and Mexico.

His books, 17 in total, have been translated into many languages. He was also the founding editor of *Share International* magazine, launched in 1982; it is circulated in over 70 countries.

He brought hope to the millions who have heard and been touched by the news of the imminent emergence of the World Teacher, and the consequent transformation of the world by the creation of justice and peace, through sharing.

Benjamin Creme lived in London where he died on 24 October 2016.

Printed in the USA
CPSIA information can be obtained
at www.ICGtesting.com
BVHW051933250823
668898BV00004B/109

9 789491 732386